A Starting-Point Guide

Nantes, France

And Day Trips to the Coast & Western Loire Valley

Barry Sanders writing as:

B G Preston

Nantes, France

Copyright © 2022 by B G Preston / Barry Sanders

All rights reserved. No part of this book may be reproduced or transmitted in any form or by any means without written permission from the author via his email address of cincy3@gmail.com or Facebook page: www.Facebook.com/BGPreston.author.

ISBN: 9798402356368

1st Edition – Updated August 2022

<u>Acknowledgements:</u> The author greatly appreciates Sandra Sanders' contributions and guidance.

<u>Photography & Maps</u>: Photos and maps in the Starting-Point Guides are a mixture of those by the author and other sources such as Shutterstock, Wikimedia, Google Earth and Google Maps. No photographs or maps in this work should be used without checking with the author first.

~ ~ ~ ~ ~ ~

Nantes' Historical Center has a lot to offer

TABLE OF CONTENTS

Preface: The "Starting-Point" Traveler 1
1: Nantes Introduction 6
2: Traveling to Nantes 16
3: When to Visit 19
4: Where to Stay 24
5: Nantes Bon Voyage Pass 36
6: Getting Around Nantes 42
7: Central Nantes Attractions 56
8: Attractions on the Edge of Nantes 83
9: Coastal Towns to Explore 91
10: Nearby Towns for Great Daytrips 106
Index 117
Starting-Point Guides 118

~ ~ ~ ~ ~ ~

Preface: The "Starting-Point" Traveler
Some General Travel Suggestions

This Starting-Point guide is intended for travelers who wish to really get to know a city/area and not just make it one quick stop on a tour through France or Europe. Oriented around the concept of using Nantes as a basecamp for several days, this

Château des ducs de Bretagne
A walled palace & fortress in the heart of Nantes

Preface

handbook provides guidance on sights both in town and nearby with the goal of allowing you to have a comprehensive experience of this beautiful city and area. The central focus or "starting-point" of this guide is the French city of Nantes which is situated on the Loire River near the northwest coast of France next to the Upper Brittany region. Nantes is well positioned to be a base-camp for explorations of this scenic area such as Rennes, portions of the Loire Valley, and delightful coastal towns such as Vannes.

This is not a complete guide to the entire Brittany (Bretagne) and **Pays de la Loire region** nor the entire northwestern area of France. Such a guide would go beyond the suggested scope of staying in one town and having enjoyable day trips from there. The area covered here is for the most popular sights which can be reached by train or car in 90 minutes or less each way.

Itinerary Ideas & Suggested Plan:

Suggested Duration: If your travel schedule allows **plan on staying 3 to 5 nights in Nantes**. This is an area with a wonderful variety of sights outside the town. Several days are needed to gain even a moderate understanding of what the region has to offer. If possible, keep a day open toward the end of your visit to tour or revisit areas which you discover during your first days in the area.

> **Nantes Tourist Office Website**
>
> www.Nantes-Tourisme.com

Visit the Tourist Office. Nantes' primary tourist office is on a popular shopping street near the notable **Château des ducs** in

A Starting-Point Guide

the heart of town. Two other offices are close to popular attractions.

The personnel in the offices (many speak English) can provide current information on available tours, transportation, and places to visit. Even if you have done substantial research prior to your trip, it is likely you will learn of additional opportunities which you had not previously uncovered.

Nantes Tourist Office

Consider a City Pass: Most cities have discount cards for visitors which can be valuable and reduce hassle if you plan on visiting several attractions. In Nantes, this helpful tool is called the **Nantes Bon Voyage Pass** or **"Pass Nantes."** See Chapter 5 for details on this card. Available in 24-, 48- and 72-hour variations, this pass can be a great help to first time visitors.

Obtain information on Local Transportation. Many European cities such as Nantes will have excellent tram and bus systems. In the case of Nantes, there is a good mix of trams and buses which will take visitors throughout the city and much of the local area.

Preface

Nantes has an excellent tram and bus network.
Photo Source: Cramos - Wikimedia

Understanding this system can be daunting at first. The staff at the Tourist Office will be able to provide help and transportation maps. See Chapter 6 for details on the area's transportation options and how to use them.

Download Some Apps:

With the incredible array of apps for Apple and Android devices, almost every detail you will need for a great trip is available up to and including where to find public toilets. One caution, several of the apps are only available in French.

Nantes Specific apps:

- **Explore Nantes:** Well produced app which provides details on Nantes' attractions, museums, restaurants and more. Detailed maps and route guidance.

- **Pass Nantes / Le Voyage a Nantes**: Provided by the City Pass providers with details on area points-of-interest and transportation guidance.

- **Nantes Tram Map**: Produced by MetroMap, a firm which provides quality transportation apps for many cities. Details on the area's tram network and schedules.

- **Nantes Bicloo:** Nantes has an excellent bike rental system, and this app guides you through renting and finding available bikes.

- **SNCF Trains**: The French train system. This app allows you to view train schedules and purchase tickets.

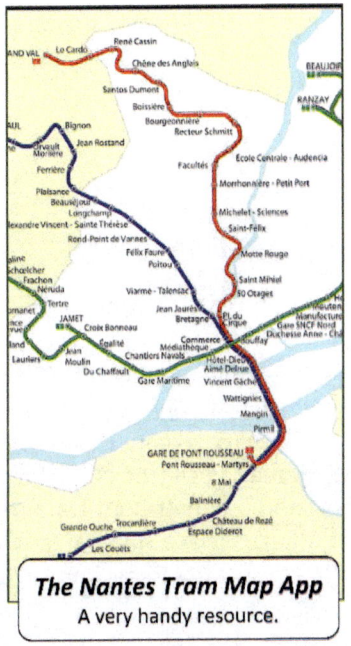

The Nantes Tram Map App
A very handy resource.

General Travel Apps:[1]

- **Rome2Rio**: An excellent way to research all travel options including rental cars, trains, flying, ferries, and taxis. The app provides the ability to purchase tickets directly online.

- **Trip Advisor**: Probably the best overall app for finding details on most hotels, restaurants, excursions, and attractions.

- **Flush**: A very helpful app which provides guidance on where to find public toilets.

~ ~ ~ ~ ~ ~

---

[1] **General Travel Apps**: There are numerous excellent travel apps to select from. The ones cited here are recommended by the author, but your search for helpful apps should not be limited to this.

1: Nantes Introduction

Nantes is the sixth largest city in France, and the westernmost of the country's cities. There is something of a feel of Paris here with the architecture, café culture, many small parks, and a notable river, the Loire, running through it.

The city largely sits off by itself and is not central to other large cities. Paris, the closest major metropolitan area, is about a two- and one-half-hour train trip away. As a result of this semi-isolation, this is a quiet area which is not overrun with tourists who are seeking to pack in several cities in a whirlwind tour.

Nantes is an easy town to explore on foot with its broad avenues and long pedestrian shopping lanes.
Photo Source: Google Maps

Nantes may not be close to large cities, but it is perfectly situated for experiencing a great variety of smaller cities such as Vannes or Angers, the coast and its many beautiful villages, area wines, and numerous historic towns and chateaux.

Nantes is the capital of the French region of Pays de la Loire.

Nantes has over 300,000 people within the city limits, and the metropolitan area is nearly one million. Even with this, the city does not feel urban or crowded. It is a city to visit to experience "the real France" not a tourist destination filled with large museums and historical monuments.

> **Nantes Accolades:**
> - Named the 2019 European Capital of Innovation.
> - Time Magazine cited Nantes as Europe's most livable city.
> - In 2013, it was awarded as the "European Green Capital" for its numerous green initiatives.

The city got its name from the Gallo-Roman name "Namnetes[2]", dating to the first century. With its position on the broad Loire River and proximity to the coast, this was a natural place

Stroll the shores of the Erdre River in central Nante. This river flows under the city into the Loire.

---

[2] **Namnetes name meaning**: Per Wikipedia, the meaning of the name is uncertain, but many believe it is derived from the Gaul language meaning "Men of the River."

Nantes Introduction

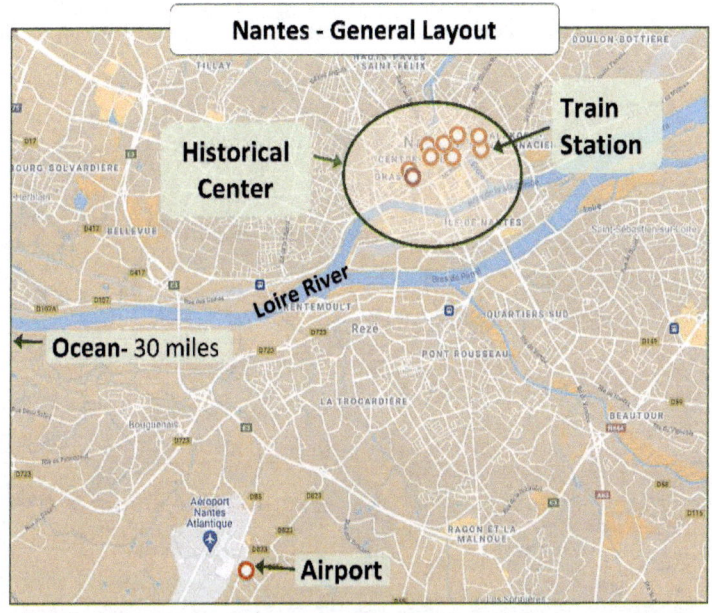

to settle. This is the capital of the French region of Pays de la Loire. The name "Pays de la Loire" means "Land of the Loire" and the region is one of 12 within mainland France. (An additional 6 regions represent the overseas territories such as Corsica.) This region borders Brittany to the northwest, Normandy to the North, and the large region of Nouvelle-Aquitaine forms much of the region's southern border.

Nantes Pronunciation
"Non t"
Or try
"Nohn t"

Nantes is an easy to reach city by train or car and flights are available from several area cities such as London, Nice, Paris, and Lyon. Information on travel into and around Nantes may be found in Chapters 2 & 6 of this guide.

A Starting-Point Guide

What to Expect When Visiting Here:

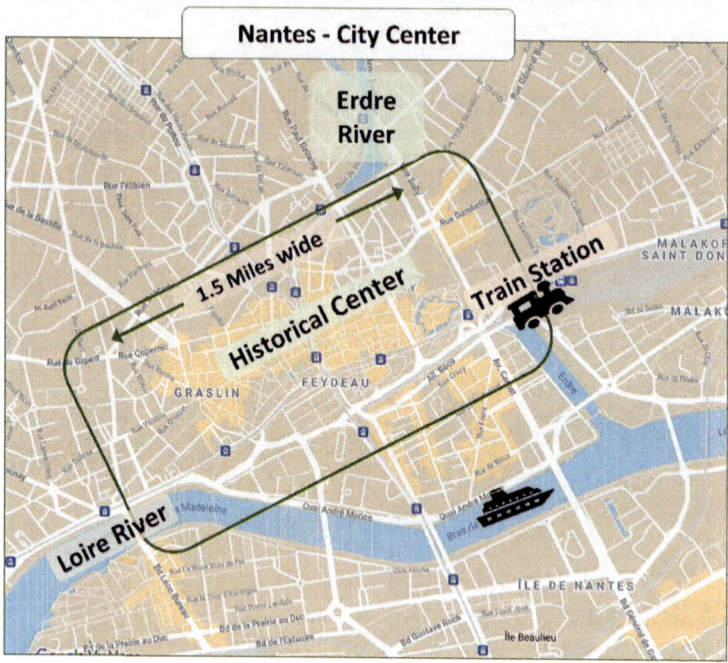

This is mostly a laid-back, small city. The city center can be busy with activity, but nowhere near the level of larger cities. Visitors will rarely feel as if they are in a mid-city crush. The numerous pedestrian streets, broad lanes, and street-side cafés make this an enjoyable area to stroll, shop, and dine.

Nantes is located on a river plain and is mostly flat. This makes getting around on foot or bicycle quite easy. The green initiatives, for which Nantes is known, make it easy to travel by local eco-friendly buses and trams. For bicyclists, there is an expansive network of bike trails, in addition to over one-hundred bike rental stations.

Nantes Introduction

This is a compact city with a good mix of history, several open plazas, and easy strolling.

Plan Around Closings:

To ensure your time in Nantes is not wasted, it is important to note the following:

Many shops are closed on Sunday.

Many museums are closed on Tuesday and some on Monday.

The architecture largely dates to the 17th through early 19th centuries with many buildings made of local sandstone and some older half-timbered structures. Few high rises are here. The general feel of the old town is similar to Paris, especially with the many Haussmann-style buildings. Much of the city center conforms to the era when this was a walled town, so most of the attractions visitors will wish to see are within this easy-to-explore section of town.

For individuals with limited mobility, the walks are mostly made of level concrete and sections of cobblestones are rare. This is largely a result of the rebuilding which occurred after WWII in where many streets and buildings were reworked.

There are few language issues for English speakers here. This region of France, Brittany and Pays de la Loire, is a very popular destination for British expats and, when strolling through the town, many bilingual signs are present.

Two different rivers form this city. The Loire splits into two arms and goes around the "Île de Nantes," and the Erdre which now travels under portions of the city. There is little along the Loire in the way of attractions, shops, or restaurants so, for most visitors, this is not high on the list of sights.

The "Île de Nantes" had been mostly an unappealing industrial area. In recent years, several projects along the northern shore are changing the island's character with several attractions and shopping areas. An homage to Jules Verne, who is from Nantes, may be found in an enjoyable amusement park located on the island.

Shopping and Dining in Nantes:

This city is a shopper's dream. The central area of town has numerous shopping lanes lined with small boutiques and even larger department stores such as Galleries Lafayette. One long set of shopping streets stretches for over a kilometer to connect the cathedral to Place Graslin the western edge of old town.

There is no one specific street to head toward for shopping as there are many interconnected pedestrian shopping lanes. A great place to start is Rue Crébillon which connects Place Royale to Place Graslin and it is the location of several designer stores. There is even the special term of **"Crébillonner"** which is the word for window shopping here.

When looking for dining which is reflective of the area, there is an interesting mix of specialties which have derived from the mix of coastal and interior influences. Many restaurants specialize in local sea food served with the area's white wines. A popular treat found in many bistros and food stalls are the "rigolettes" which are fruit-filled cakes and biscuits.

Interested in wine? Several stores (caves) specializing in Loire Valley wines may be found in central Nantes.

Some History:

Like many cities, Nantes was developed around commerce and access to shipping. For centuries, ships would sail up the estuary from the ocean, up the Loire, and dock at Nantes. The port here was one of the most active in Europe. The Erdre River emptied into the Loire at this point, helping commerce even more. Later, as ships grew bigger, much of this activity was moved to the coast.

The Memorial to the Abolition of Slavery
"Mémorial de L'abolition de L'esclavage"

Nantes was a part of the Breton dukedom. This is very evident by the large castle and palace in the center of town. The region was able to remain independent until the 16th century when it became part of the French kingdom.

Much of the local economy during the 16th and 17th centuries was built around exports of wine, fabrics, and salt. With good harbors along the Loire, local merchants were able to easily transport these products until shipping was moved to the coastal towns.

A dark part of Nantes' history is the slave trade with America. This port actively engaged in shipping slaves to North America well after all other ports and regions had ceased this activity. There were an estimated 400,000 slaves shipped out of this region during the 18th and 19th century period of slave trading. A large monument to the end of this trade sits along the Loire River on the Île de Nantes.

The Area Close to Central Nantes:

A beach park at Saint-Nazaire
Several coastal towns near Nantes provide for relaxing getaways.

Nantes Introduction

The Pays de la Loire region neighboring Nantes is a mix of rolling hills, vineyards, and other agriculture, several notable chateaux, natural parks, and the numerous coastal towns. Attractions include western sections of the Loire Valley[3] and seaside resorts including Saint-Nazaire and Pornichet. Chapters 9 & 10 provide details on these destinations.

It is a great area to explore and obtain a variety of experiences. Many nearby towns will require travel by car, but some locations may be reached by the train network.

~ ~ ~ ~ ~ ~

---

[3] **Loire Valley travel from Nantes:** While there are a few tours of the Loire Valley out of Nantes, this is generally not advised as the most popular and historic Châteaux are nearly two-hours away by car. The best day trips out of Nantes are generally to the seaside towns and villages.

2: Traveling to Nantes

Nantes sits off to the northwestern sector of France and, as a result, is not a central hub of transportation. Still, traveling to Nantes is easy to reach by airplane or train. It is even a popular destination from the U.K. with many travelers taking a combination of ferry and train.

Gare de Nantes
The train station is close to the center of Nantes' old town.
Photo Source: Google Earth

The train station is right in town, requiring little extra travel once you arrive. The airport is less than 20 minutes south of town. The city's excellent transportation system connects directly to the terminals of the train and airport.

Arriving by Train

The main train station, Gare de Nantes, is very convenient to the center of town. If you have booked lodging in the heart of Nantes, you may be able to walk to there from the station. Most locations in central Nantes can be reached in less than a 20-minute walk.

The station services the high-speed system (TGV) and regional trains as well. All train travel into and out of Nantes will likely be through this station. Direct trains may be taken both to and from central Paris and the Charles-de-Gaulle airport in Paris. Travel time from central Paris on the TGV is typically under 2 ½ hours. Travel time to the Paris airport is closer to 3 hours each way.

Directly outside of the station are stops for the local tram and bus network. In addition, if you wish to make a connection with a flight, there is a shuttle, the Tan Air service, which connects the train station to the airport.

Flying to Nantes:

The Nantes airport, "Nantes Atlantique Airport", is a midsize regional airport. The airport is served by several airlines including Air France, Ryanair, Finnair, KLM and others. A majority of the flights coming into Nantes are from one of the two Paris airports with flight time of slightly over one hour.

No direct flights from North America come into this airport. When traveling from the U.S. or Canada, it is best to travel through Paris. From CDG, the Charles de Gaulle airport, there are two easy options of either taking a train directly from the airport (recommended), or catching a local flight into Nantes.

There are several options for traveling into town from the Nantes airport. No tram service the airport, but it is well serviced by the local bus system. Driving distance is 7.5 miles (around 4 miles as the crow flies), but the roads are a bit more circuitous. The 'Tan Air' shuttle departs every 30 minutes from

A Starting-Point Guide

the airport and goes directly to the Nantes train station. Cost is 9 Euro. Tickets may be purchased directly from the driver.

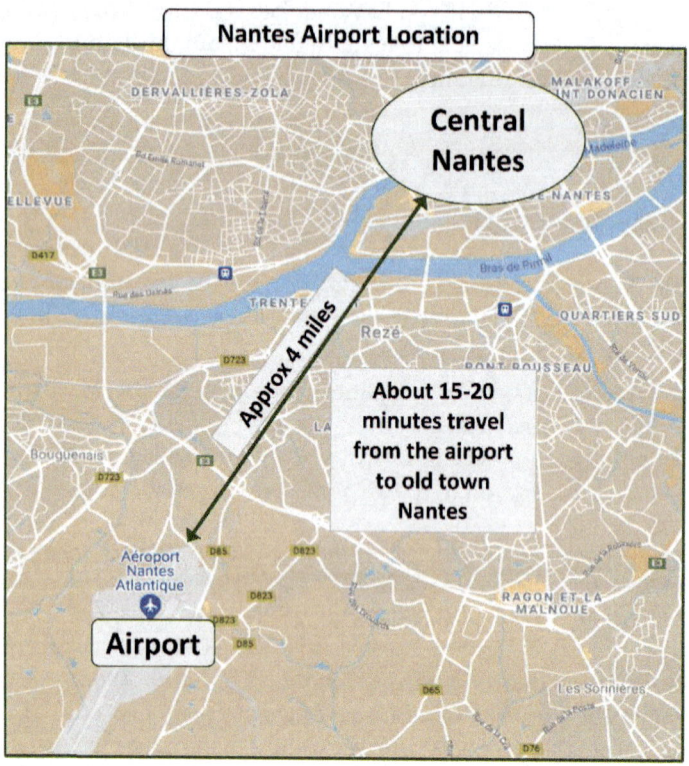

Taxi cost will run around 30 Euro depending on your destination in town. The huge advantage here is you will be taken directly to your lodging in town as opposed to the shuttle which drops you at the train station. Check **www.AirportsTaxiTransfers.com** for exact rates and you may also make a reservation through this site.

3: When to Visit

Like most areas in Europe, your best times to visit northwestern France are late Spring, early Summer, and Fall. This holds true especially if you wish to avoid crowds, enjoy touring, want to get out into the country to explore the natural attractions, or spend time on the area beaches.

Tourist Crowds:

Nantes is not high on most lists of cities to visit in France for North Americans. For individuals coming from France, the coastal area has been rapidly growing in popularity during recent years. The peak tourist season is generally in the summer months.

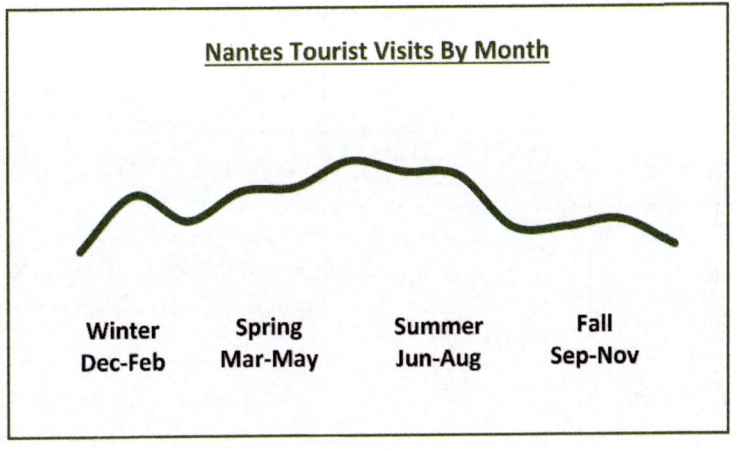

A Starting-Point Guide

Most "Top 10" lists do not include Nantes. This is actually a great aspect of this mid-size city as it is rarely overrun with tourist crowds and the attractions are more available to visit and explore. The area is popular for French and British visitors as the climate provides enjoyable and relaxing vacations. For Parisians, the area is a popular city-break destination.

Local Climate:

The northwest of France has an oceanic climate which can bring in light rains all year. Temperatures are the most pleasant during the late spring and summer months and are rarely overly hot. This climate lends itself to enjoyable days of relaxing strolls and days on the beach.

In the winter, the cold ocean winds can be unpleasant, although generally not freezing. With most tourists gone during this time of the year, many shops, services, and tours will be closed.

Average Nantes Climate by Month				
Month		Avg High	Avg Low	Avg Rain
Jan	☹	48 F / 9 C	38 F / 3 C	3.4 inches
Feb	☹	50 F / 10 C	37 F / 3 C	2.7 inches
Mar	😐	55 F / 13 C	41 F / 5 C	2.4 inches
Apr	😐	60 F / 16 C	44 F / 6 C	2.4 inches

When to Visit

Average Nantes Climate by Month				
Month		Avg High	Avg Low	Avg Rain
May	☺	67 F / 19 C	50 F / 10 C	2.6 inches
Jun	☺	73 F / 23 C	55 F / 13 C	1.7 inches
Jul	😐	77 F / 25 C	58 F / 14 C	1.8 inches
Aug	😐	77 F / 25 C	57 F / 14 C	1.7 inches
Sep	☺	72 F / 22 C	53 F / 2 C	2.5 inches
Oct	☺	64 F / 18 C	49 F / 9 C	3.6 inches
Nov	😐	54 F / 12 C	42 F / 8 C	3.5 inches
Dec	☹	49 F / 9 C	38 F / 3 C	3.8 inches

~ ~ ~ ~ ~ ~

Major Festivals & Events in Nantes:

There are several popular events in and near Nantes each year. Visiting one of these can be a great addition in a visit to the area. The only moderate downsides are the added crowds and increased lodging rates. Information on some of the leading events follow. This is not a complete list of all events in and near Nantes.

Classical Musical Festival / La Folle Journee: For lovers of great music, this event is a must see. The focus on this popular set of concerts is on noted classical composers. Numerous musicians and musical groups come to play music which is geared to a different composer each year. The focus of the 2022 season, for example, is on Schubert.

- Timing: Held late each January or early February and lasts for 4 to 5 days. Advance purchase of tickets is recommended.
- Location: Several venues are utilized both in Nantes and in the surrounding area. The larger events are held in the Cité des Congrés (Nantes Convention Center) which is located on the Erdre River near the confluence with the Loire.
- Website: **www.Jds.fr/Nantes** (Then follow the links to info on this event)

Hip Opsession / Festival Hip Opsession: A lively event with a focus on the hip-hop culture. Hundreds of dance and music performers in dozens of concerts city wide.

- Timing: Generally held in late February or early March.
- Website: **www.HipOpsession.com**

HellFest /Metalfest: An open-air festival for ultra-modern music including punk, metal, grind, and more. Over 100 bands performing with more than 100,000 people attending this one-week event.

When to Visit

- Location: Held in the town of Clisson, which is 30-minutes southeast from central Nantes. Trains regularly service this route.
- Timing: mid-June.
- Website: **www.MetalfestEurope.com** - then follow the links to Hellfest.

3 Continents Festival / Festival des 3 Continents: A popular cinema festival with showings representing Africa, Asia, and Latin America.

Location: Film screenings are held in multiple locations in Nantes and around the region. Check the website for all sites in which films will be shown.

Timing: mid to late November.

Website: **www.3Continents.com**.

Nantes Christmas Market / Marché de Noël à Nantes: The largest Christmas market in western France. Over 100 vendors and numerous musical events. A fun place to browse, especially at night when the cathedral and much of the historic center is fully lit for the holidays.

- Timing: Held from mid-November until December 22nd. (Dates may vary slightly each year). Hours are from mid-morning until 8PM or 9PM depending on the day you arrive.
- Location: The event largely takes over the historical center with booth and activities in the large Place Royale and Place du Commerce and several spots in between.
- Website: **www.Nantes-Tourisme.com** (Then follow the links to info on this event)

~ ~ ~ ~ ~ ~

4: Where to Stay

Where you choose to stay when visiting a new city is essentially a personal choice. You may prefer hotels or rental apartments. Picking a place guided by your budget may be critical to you.

Regardless of the motives which drive your selection of accommodation type, the "Where in town should I stay?" question is critical to helping you have an enjoyable visit.

Budget and accommodation-type issues aside, the following criteria may be of importance to you:

- Convenience to historical sites, restaurants, shopping.
- Convenience to transportation.
- Noise levels around where you will stay.

This guide does not provide details on all hotels in Nantes. There are simply too many to describe, and there are many areas to consider. There are many fine and dynamic online sources such as **Booking.com** or **Trip Advisor** [4] which give far more detail than can be

> **Author's Suggestion:**
>
> Stay in the old town area (Historical center) and not in one of neighboring areas.

---

[4] **Hotel Ratings**: All hotel ratings cited in this chapter are a blend from several sources such as Booking.com, Hotels.com, and Trip Advisor as of mid-2022.

Where to Stay

provided here. These sites will provide answers to every question about a property you are considering and allow you to make reservations once you have made your selection. Another great resource is the Nantes Tourist Office website. **Nantes-Tourisme.com.**

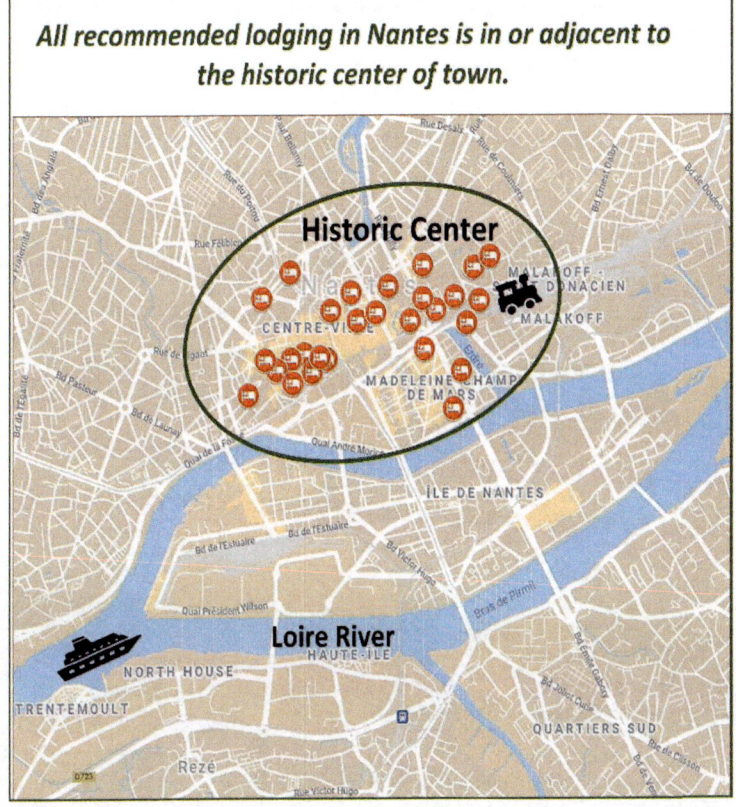

All recommended lodging in Nantes is in or adjacent to the historic center of town.

A Starting-Point Guide

Recommended Lodging Area:

Quality lodging may be found throughout the metropolitan area including the Nantes suburbs, the airport, and neighboring towns. For first time visitors, unless you have a specific destination outside the city center, it is recommended that you stay in or close to the historic center. All lodging categories such as hotels, inns, B&B, and Air B&B accommodations may be found here. This guide focuses on hotels and inns only.

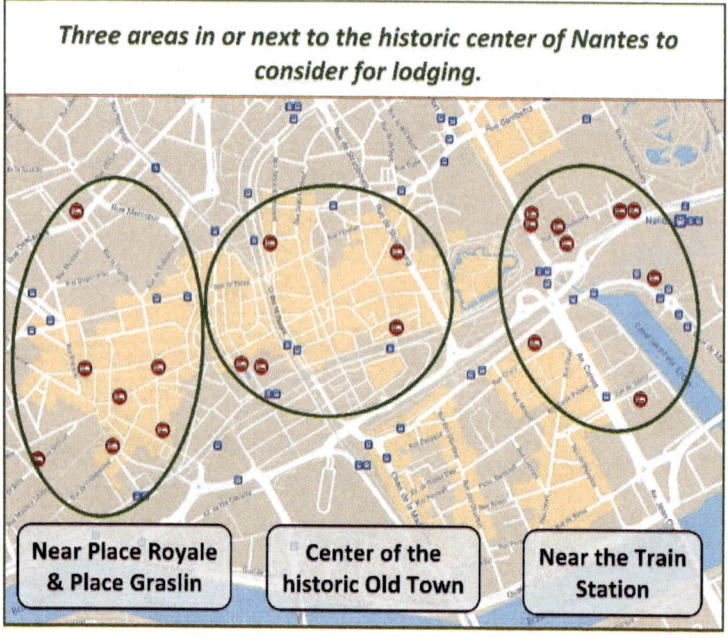

Three areas in or next to the historic center of Nantes to consider for lodging.

- Near Place Royale & Place Graslin
- Center of the historic Old Town
- Near the Train Station

There are three sections of town to consider here. Each has its own set of advantages. (a) Near the train station, (b) in the center of the historic area, or (c) near Place Royale.

Where to Stay

Near the Train Station: This is the area within a short walk from the train station. In this section of town, there are several properties across from the train station, near the large botanical garden (Jardin des Plantes) and close to the Bretagne Chateau. Several lodging options may also be found near the River Erdre and the marina.

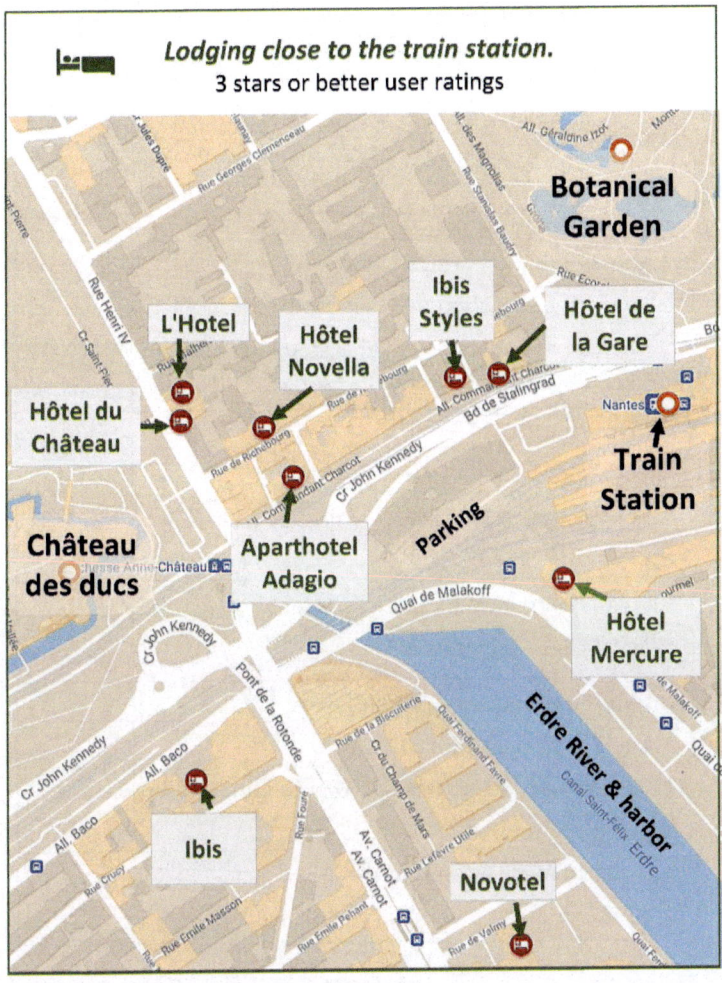

A Starting-Point Guide

For visitors who want easy access to the heart of town and who are likely to take several day trips by train, this is area should be considered. One additional advantage to this section of town is immediate access to the town's local transportation network. See Chapter 6 for details on this system. Walking time into the heart of the historic center and its many shops and restaurants will be 10+ minutes each way.

Hotels near the Nantes Train Station	
User ratings of 3 stars or greater. Ratings are a composite of popular sources including: Booking.com, Hotels.com & Trip Advisor.	
Hotel Name & Website	**Rating**
Aparthotel Adagio Nantes Centre - www.Adagio-City.com – then search for Nantes - There is more than one "Aparthotel" in Nantes. This is the only one using the "Adagio" title.	4 stars
Hôtel Du Château - www.Hotel-Du-Chateau-Nantes.fr - Immediately across from the noted Château des ducs de Bretagne.	3.5 stars
Hôtel de la Gare Nantes Logis Citotel - Hotel-Gare-Nantes.com	3.5 stars
Hôtel Mercure Nantes Centre Gare - Hotel-Mercure-Nantes.com - New property set off from the central area, next to the marina.	4 stars
Ibis Nantes Centre Gare Sud (South) - All.Accor.com – then search for Nantes	4 stars

Hotels near the Nantes Train Station

User ratings of 3 stars or greater. Ratings are a composite of popular sources including: Booking.com, Hotels.com & Trip Advisor.

Hotel Name & Website	Rating
- Large, somewhat newer property.	
Ibis Styles Nantes Centre Gare - All.Accor.com – then search for Nantes - Located immediately across from the train station.	4 stars
Inter-Hotel Novella Nantes Centre Gare - Also cited as "The Originals City, Hôtel Novella - www.Novella-Nantes-Centre.com	3.5 stars
L'Hotel - www.NantesHotel.com - Mid-size boutique hotel	3.5 stars
Novotel Nantes Centre Gare - Also cited as Hôtel Novotel Nantes Centre Gare - All.Accor.com – then search for Nantes - Property is convenient to the Erdre and Loire	4 stars

~ ~ ~ ~ ~ ~

Lodging in the historic center: The heart of Nantes, the Bouffay district, puts visitors in the center of a delightful maze of streets with numerous stores, bars, and restaurants.

The noted pedestrian street, Rue de la Marne, provides endless shopping opportunities including larger department stores such as Galleries Lafayette. Many of the more popular attractions such as the Château des ducs and Cathédrale Saint-Pierre are here.

A small number of well-rated boutique inns and mid-size hotels are in this sector of town. The distance to the train station, depending on the hotel, will be around 10 to 20 minutes. Stay here if you wish to be right in the center of it all.

Lobby of the Mercure Centre Grand Hôtel. A 4-star+ full-service hotel in the heart of town.

Where to Stay

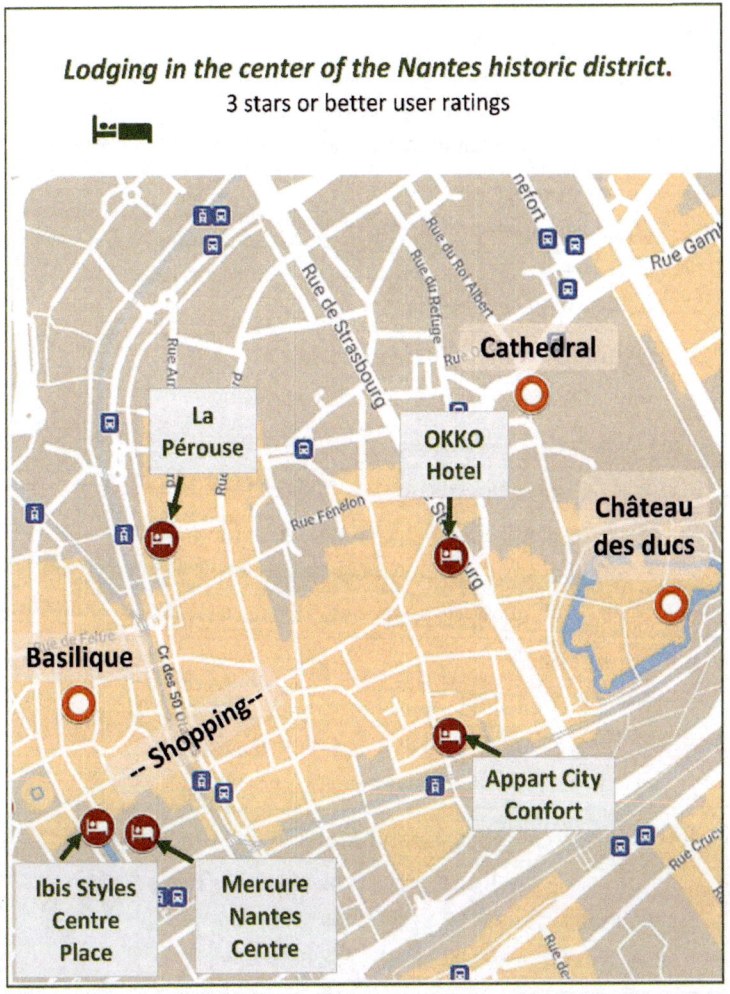

Hotels in the Center of the Historic Old Town

User ratings of 3 stars or greater. Ratings are a composite of popular sources including: Booking.com, Hotels.com & Trip Advisor.

Hotel Name & Website	Rating
Apart City Confort Nantes Centre - www.Adagio-City.com – then search for Nantes. There are several properties with "Apart Hotels" in their name in Nantes.	3 stars
OKKO Hotels Nantes Château - www.OkkoHotels.com – then select Nantes - Good central location.	4 stars
Ibis Styles Centre Place Royale - All.Accor.com – then search for Nantes. There are several Ibis Styles properties in Nantes. - Good location next to shops and a small park.	3.5 stars
La Pérouse Hôtel - www.Hotel-LaPérouse.fr - Modern property with easy access to the heart of Old Town and the tram system.	4 stars
Mercure Nantes Centre Grand Hôtel - All.Accor.com – then search for Nantes. Note there are multiple Mercure hotel properties in the area. - Large, modern hotel with all desired conveniences.	4 stars

Where to Stay

Lodging near the Place Royale or Place Graslin: The "Centre-Ville" section of town borders the Bouffay district and is a center for shopping and dining along with several business

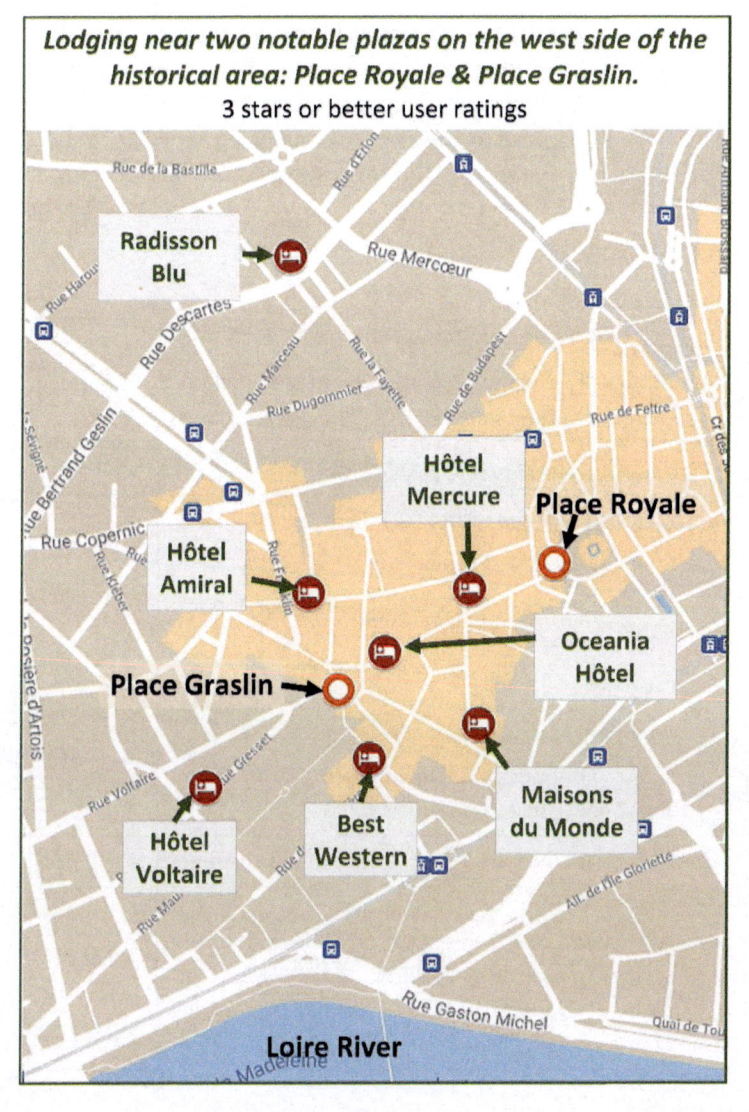

Lodging near two notable plazas on the west side of the historical area: Place Royale & Place Graslin.
3 stars or better user ratings

buildings. The city's one large office tower stands tall along the northern edge of this area.

Like the Bouffay area, there are long pedestrian shopping streets here. There are also several popular sites such as the Natural History and History museums. One popular attraction here is the "Passage Pommeraye," an ornate shopping mall built in the 1840's renaissance style.

This section is close to the city's excellent transportation network, but a fair distance to the train station. To catch a train, it is generally advised to take a local tram as walking can be over 20 minutes.

Hotels near Place Royale or Place Graslin	
User ratings of 3 stars or greater. Ratings are a composite of popular sources including: Booking.com, Hotels.com and Trip Advisor.	
Hotel Name & Website	Rating
Best Western Nantes Hôtel Graslin - www.Hotel-Graslin.com - Well located near Place Graslin and many shops and restaurants.	3.5 stars
Hôtel Amiral - www.Hotel-Nantes.fr - Midsize boutique hotel. In summer, be sure to ask for a room with A/C.	3.5 stars
Hôtel Mercure Nantes Centre Passage Pommeraye - All.Accor.com – then search for Nantes. There are several properties with the "Hotel Mercure" name in Nantes Watch for the name "Passage Pommeraye."	3.5 stars

Where to Stay

Hotels near Place Royale or Place Graslin	
User ratings of 3 stars or greater. Ratings are a composite of popular sources including: Booking.com, Hotels.com and Trip Advisor.	
Hotel Name & Website	**Rating**
Hôtel Voltaire Opera Nantes Centre - www.HotelVoltaireOperaNantes.com - Boutique hotel in a moderately quiet area, a short walk from Place Graslin	4.5 stars
Maisons du Monde Hôtel & Suites - www.MaisonsDuMondeHotel.com. - Elegant mid-size property between Place Royale and Place Graslin.	4 stars
Oceania Hôtel de France Nantes - www.OceaniaHotels.com – then search for Nantes - Recently renovated, upscale hotel.	4.5 stars
Radisson Blu Hotel Nantes - www.RadissonHotels.com–then search for Nantes - Built in an historic Court of Justice building. Slightly outside of the prime historic area.	4.5 stars

~ ~ ~ ~ ~ ~

5: Nantes Bon Voyage Pass

A Convenient Way to Discover the City & Area

If you will be staying in Nantes for several days and wish to visit multiple attractions, then acquiring a city pass, the **"Pass Nantes Bon Voyage Card,"** can be a good idea.

Nantes like most cities in Europe, offer city passes and they provide discounted or free admissions to many attractions. In Nantes, the pass includes access to nearly 40 museums, tours, and notable sites. It also includes free use of the local transportation system.

Full details on this pass and what it covers may be found at **www.Nantes-Tourisme.com**.

A potentially huge advantage is the pass **includes local transportation**. If you are likely to use this system, this can be a hassle and cost saver.

The Nantes Bon Voyage Pass is available in 24-hour, 48-hour, 72-hour, & 7-day versions.

Nantes Bon Voyage Pass

Pass Options Available:

The Pass Nantes is available in four different durations and 3 different price tiers:
- Adult rate
- Child and Student Rate
- Family Card. This pass covers two adults and two children.

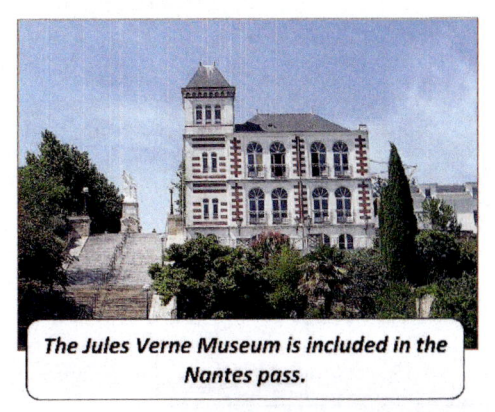

The Jules Verne Museum is included in the Nantes pass.

The passes may be purchased online or from the tourist office. When purchasing online, discounts are available, but you are required to indicate a start date for when the pass will become valid.

Each pass is available for a consecutive period of 24-hours, 48-hours, 72-hours, or one week. It does not accommodate the ability to select non-consecutive days such as using a 48-hour card for a Tuesday and a Friday.

When purchasing passes online, you may select to either have them mailed to you or to be picked up at the tourist office in town or the airport.

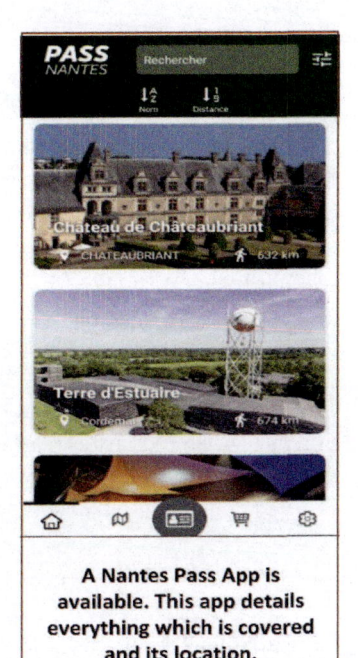

A Nantes Pass App is available. This app details everything which is covered and its location.

A Starting-Point Guide

Pass Pricing

Nantes Pass Pricing: [5]			
Below is online pricing. Fares may be slightly more when purchased directly from the Tourist Office.			
Duration	Adult Rate	Child Rate	Family Pass (2 adults + 2 children)
24-Hour	26€	18€	70€
48-Hour	35€	25€	95€
72-Hour	45€	32€	122€
7-Days	90€	60€	240€

What is Included:

The passes include a mix of free and discounted items. The following table outlines most of the attractions which are covered. Note that, with the exception of city transportation, a pass may be used only once to obtain free admission or the eligible discount.

The 7-day pass includes some items which are not part of the 24-, 48-, or 72-hour passes.

Some attractions such as the Erdre River Cruise and the City Tour Bus require that booking to be made directly at the Tourist Office in Nantes. Details on this and all specific requirements are detailed in the app.

---

[5] **Price Note:** Pricing cited here is from July-2022 and is subject to change. Check with **www.Nantes-Tourisme.com** or the Tourist Office while in Nantes for current pass cost.

What the Nantes Passes Include

Group	Attraction	24-, 48- or 72-Hour Pass	7-Day Pass
Transportation & Tour Buses	Light Rail	Unlimited Use	
	City Buses	Unlimited Use	
	Bicycle Rental		
	E-Bike Rental	Not Included	Included
	River Shuttles on the Erdre and Loire	Included	
	Local Train to Several Nearby Towns	Not Included	Various Discounts
Museums	Fine Arts Museum	Included	
	Dukes of Brittany Castle	Included	
	Jules Verne Museum	Included	

What the Nantes Passes Include

Group	Attraction	24-, 48- or 72-Hour Pass	7-Day Pass
	History Museum	Included	
	Nantes Printing Museum	Included	
Local Attractions	Gallery of the Island Machines	Included	
	Sea World Merry-Go-Round	Included	
	Planetarium	Included	
	Art Exhibits	Several exhibits in leading museums offer free entrance to Nantes Pass Holders.	
Tours	Audio Guided Tour	Included	
	Erdre River Cruise	Included	
	City Tour Bus	Included	

Nantes Bon Voyage Pass

Group	Attraction	24-, 48- or 72-Hour Pass	7-Day Pass
	Segway Tour	Included	
	Tourist Train	Included	
	Loire River Cruise	Not Included	Included
Dining	Various	Several restaurants offer a free desert or other item to Nantes Pass holders.	
Near Nantes Attractions (Sample List – there are numerous attractions near Nantes included in the pass)	Mini-Golf	Included	
	Le Chronographe Archeological Site in Rezé.	Included	
	Clisson Castle in Clisson	Included	
	La Garenne Lemont Estate	Included	
	Coing Castle	Included	

~ ~ ~ ~ ~ ~

6: Getting Around Nantes

Walking, Trams, Buses, Bikes, & River Shuttles

The center of Nantes is level and relatively easy to find your way around. The Old Town area is a pleasant maze of small streets but, for most individuals, navigating the area will not be a challenge. Nantes is very pedestrian oriented and there are several streets which are reserved for pedestrian use.

The most popular attractions are a mix of those located right in the heart of the historic district and those that are a short way out such as the sights found on the Île de Nantes. To reach the more popular destinations, a mix of walking and taking the local trams will probably be needed for most individuals.

When staying here, there is little need to have a car in town or for travel to the more popular out-of-town locales such as the coastal towns. The train system is excellent and most popular destinations can be reached by train or bus.

In Nantes, you have numerous travel options including bicycle rental and even several river shuttles/ferries. Most means of transportation (excluding taxis) are covered by the Nantes Pass.

If you are staying in central Nantes, walking distances from your lodging to most popular attractions, restaurants, and shops is less than a 20-minute jaunt and most of this is along level streets. One caution is that several of the smaller streets have cobblestones which can be problematic to individuals with impaired mobility.

Getting Around Nantes

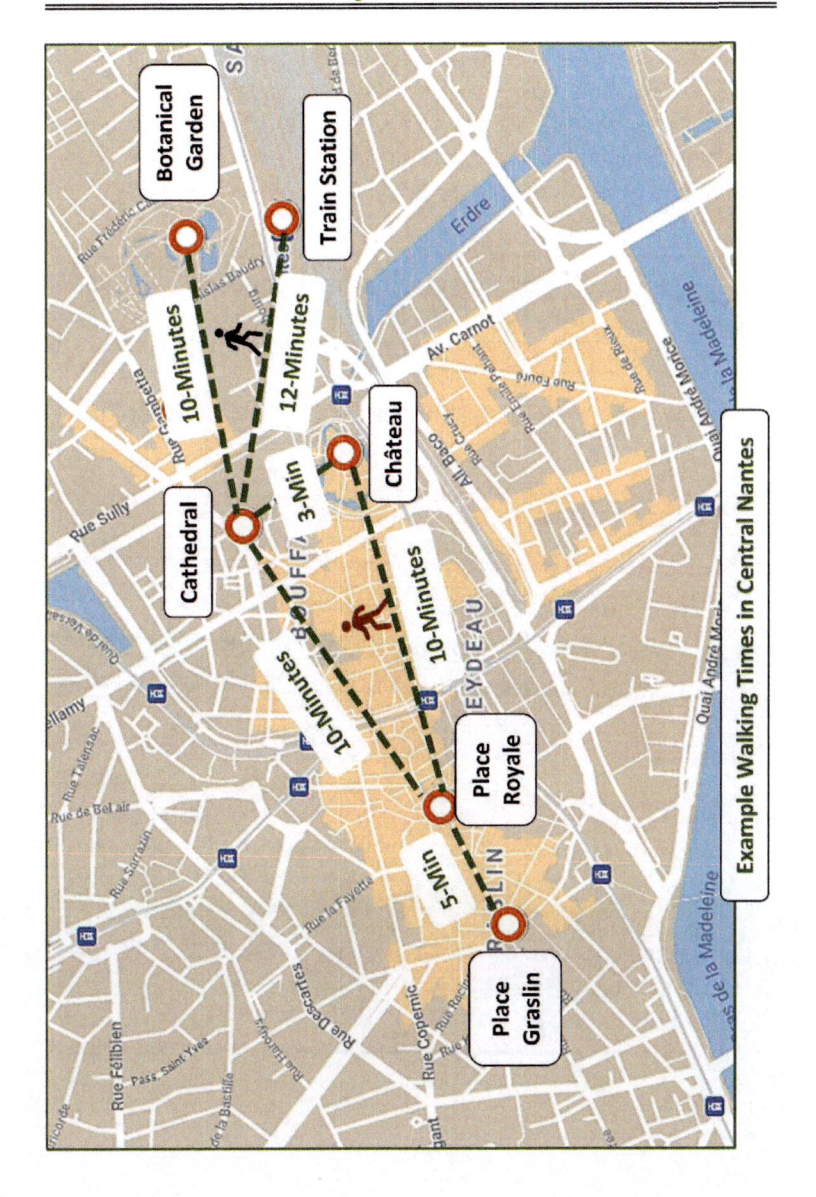

Example Walking Times in Central Nantes

A Starting-Point Guide

Some attractions such as the Jules Verne Museum and the Carousel on the Île de Nantes[6] are within walking distance although it can be a bit of a hike. Travel to these locations is generally best done on local transportation if for no other reason than traffic along the routes can be busy.

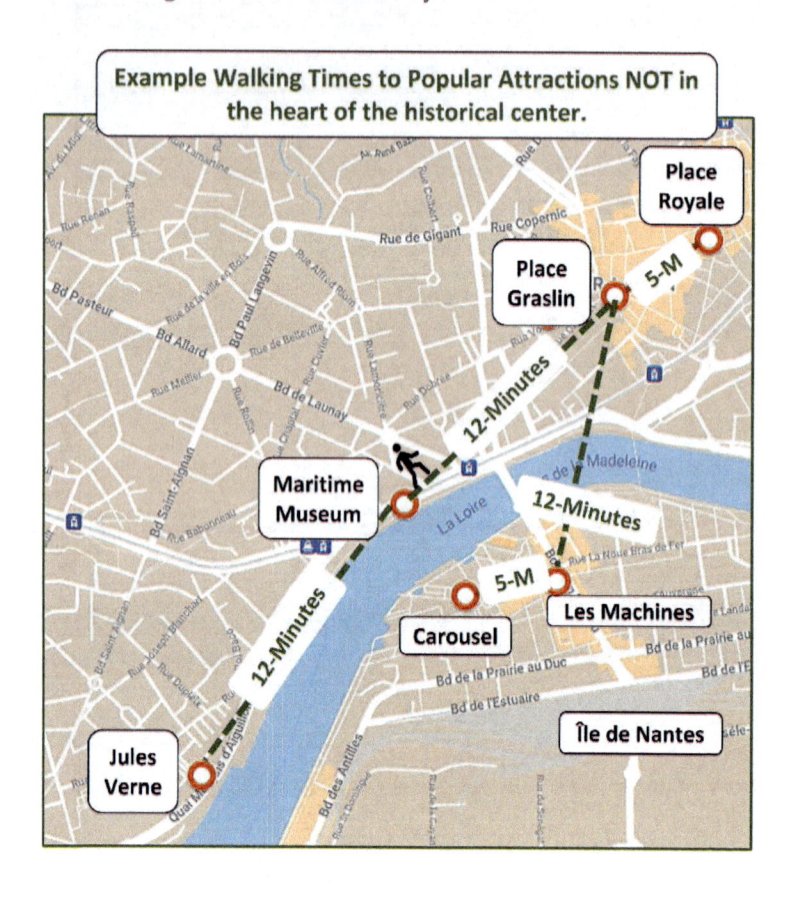

Example Walking Times to Popular Attractions NOT in the heart of the historical center.

---

[6] **Île de Nantes:** The island area across the Loire River from the Nantes historical center.

44

Getting Around Nantes

The Nantes Transportation System Apps and Tickets:

TAN is the name for the transportation system in Nantes. It includes a comprehensive mix of trams, buses, and even river shuttles. An important reminder regarding this system **is that it is free to use if you have a Nantes Pass.**

One exception is the airport shuttle. These shuttles are not included in the daily tickets or Nantes Pass. Shuttle tickets may be purchased separately via the website, app, or at the departure point.

Website: The website for this system is **www.Tan.fr**. The site includes full details on routes, fares, and timetables. You may also purchase tickets from this site.

App: Also, consider downloading the TAN app. The official app is titled "Tan" or "Réseau Tan." Other apps are also available. This app provides the same level of route and timetable detail as the website.

The TAN (Nantes Transportation) app provides full details on the local system. Available in English

Ticket Duration Options: Several choices are available to provide different amounts of time or number of rides covered. These include:

- 1-Hour Tickets. Unlimited rides during a 1-hour period starting from when you first board the tram or bus.

- 10-Ticket Booklets: Ten 1-hour trips may be taken- with a discount fee per trip.

A Starting-Point Guide

- <u>24-Hour Pass</u>: Good for unlimited use over a 24-hour period, starting from when the pass was first used.

- <u>Airport Shuttle</u>: Tickets for the airport shuttle from the train station are purchased separately.

- <u>Longer Periods</u>. If you plan on staying in the area for a month or more, discounted tickets may be purchased for a month or more with unlimited usage.

Ticket Purchase Points: All TAN system tickets may be purchased: online, via the App, at ticket kiosks found at every tram and river shuttle stop, most bus stops. Several local resellers in town also sell these passes.

When purchasing tickets from the kiosks, you may use either cash or credit cards.

Ticket Costs: Tickets cover transportation on all public modes of transportation and there is no need to purchase separate tickets for buses or trams and river shuttles. (As of mid-2022 and subject to change.)

- o 1-Hour Ticket: 1,70€
- o 10-Ticket Booklet: 16€
- o 24-Hour Pass 6€
- o 24-Hour Pass for 4 people 11€

> **Free on Weekends!**
>
> Fun fact... you may ride the local buses, trams, and river shuttles at no cost on weekends. No tickets or passes are required.

~ ~ ~ ~ ~ ~

The Nantes Tram System/Tramway de Nantes:

An integral component of the Nantes transportation system are the trams. The tram system in Nantes is generally easy to learn as there are only 3 lines and they are numbered simply "1, 2, and 3." All three of the lines travel through the heart of Nantes and meet roughly in the mid-point of the historic district.

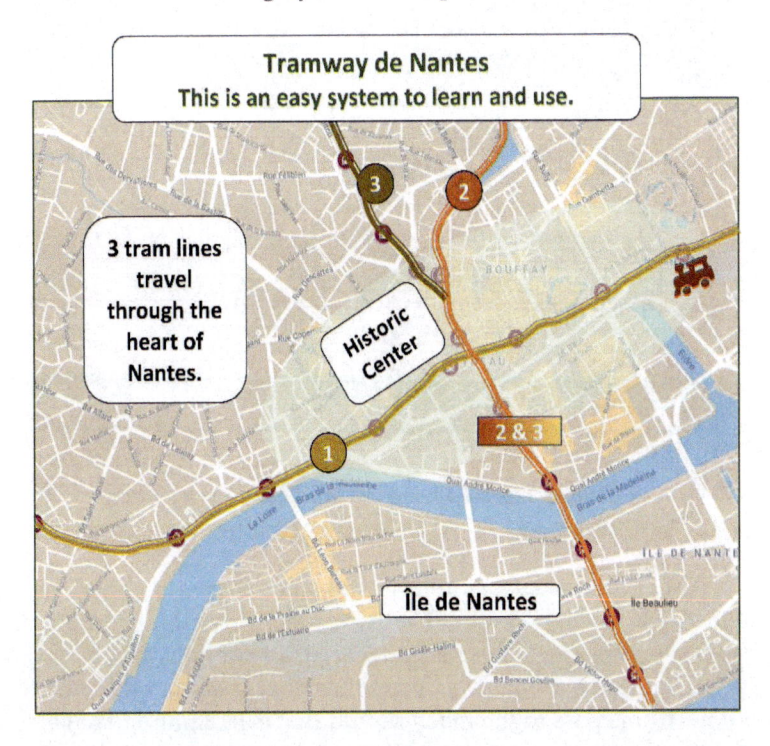

Tramway de Nantes
This is an easy system to learn and use.

3 tram lines travel through the heart of Nantes.

Historic Center

Île de Nantes

The one downside to this that many of the most popular attractions, such as those located on the Île de Nantes (Les Machines and Carousel) are not directly connected to the trams. The extensive bus system does directly connect to most of the tram stops, making a complete trip to any attraction easy via a mix of tram and bus.

A Starting-Point Guide

The previous graph only shows the stops in or close to the city center. The three lines of the tram system go far beyond the historical area and cover much of the Nantes suburbs. Full maps of the system are available on the system's website, app, and are detailed at every tram stop in the system.

A Nantes Tram Passing By the Château des ducs.

Using the tickets is simple. First, you must have a valid pass, either one purchased specifically for the Nantes transportation system or a Nantes Pass. Second, each tram and bus will have a ticket validator available as you enter. Present either the paper or electronic pass to the machine and that is it. Failure to have a ticket validated can result in a fine.

~ ~ ~ ~ ~

Getting Around Nantes

Navibus River Shuttles:

The Navibus river shuttles provide a fun way to travel from central Nantes to other areas of town such as the Île de Nantes.

Riding the Navibus is included in the Nantes Pass and in any of the Nantes transportation passes such as the 24-Hour pass.

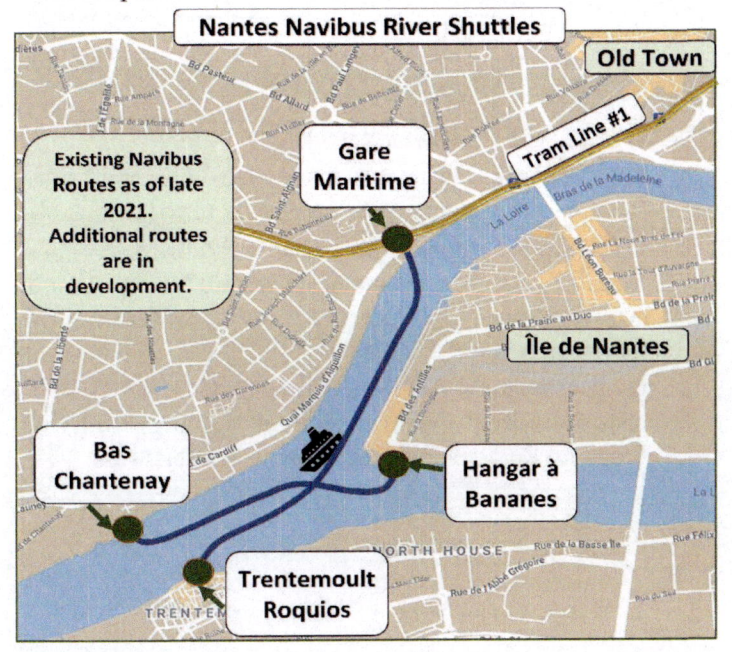

A fun way to explore the area is the Navibus river shuttle.
Photo Source: Wikimedia

Nantes Navibus River Shuttles

- Old Town
- Gare Maritime
- Tram Line #1
- Île de Nantes
- Bas Chantenay
- Hangar à Bananes
- Trentemoult Roquios

Existing Navibus Routes as of late 2021. Additional routes are in development.

49

A Starting-Point Guide

Navibus Routes & Ports: As of this writing there are just two routes servicing a total of four stops. More routes, designed to increase convenience to the Île de Nantes, are in development and may be available in late 2022 or early 2023.

- Gare Maritime to Trentemoult Roquios.
    - This route is recommended for casual visitors who simply want to explore some more of the area in a relaxing fashion
    - Gare Maritime is the closest to the heart of Nantes and is easy to reach by taking Tram line #1 and exiting at the "Gare Maritime" tram stop. From there it is a short walk across a highway to the dock. This Navibus dock is adjacent to the Maritime Museum where you can go aboard a retired navy destroyer.
    - Trentemount Roquios. This is a colorful village across the Loire from central Nantes with many small restaurants. A bicycle rental stand is adjacent to the Navibus dock.

- Bas Chantenay to Hangar à Bananes (Île de Nantes)
    - This route takes visitors to the Île de Nantes and brings them within walking distance of several attractions.
    - Bas Chantenay dock is not connected to the tram lines. It may be reached by taking buses 10, 81, or C1 from central Nantes. The dock is a 5-minute walk from the bus stop.
    - Hangar à Bananas on Île de Nantes is near the "Les Anneaux de Buren" walkway with colorful rings bordering the Loire River. Several restaurants line this walk.

~ ~ ~ ~ ~

Getting Around Nantes

City Tour Bus:

A relaxing mode of viewing the city is to take the "City Tour Bus." This is provided in a mid-size convertible bus which opens in good weather. Tours are provided in several languages via headset and provide historical background on the area and attractions.

The tour duration is 75 minutes and provides details on over 20 of the city's leading sights (see the following map and list). You do not leave the bus during the tour, nor do you go into any of the attractions.

> **Not a "Hop-On/Hop-Off" Tour**
>
> The Nantes City Tour Bus does **not** stop to let riders off at any of the sights along the way. Once you board, you are expected to complete the 75-minute journey.

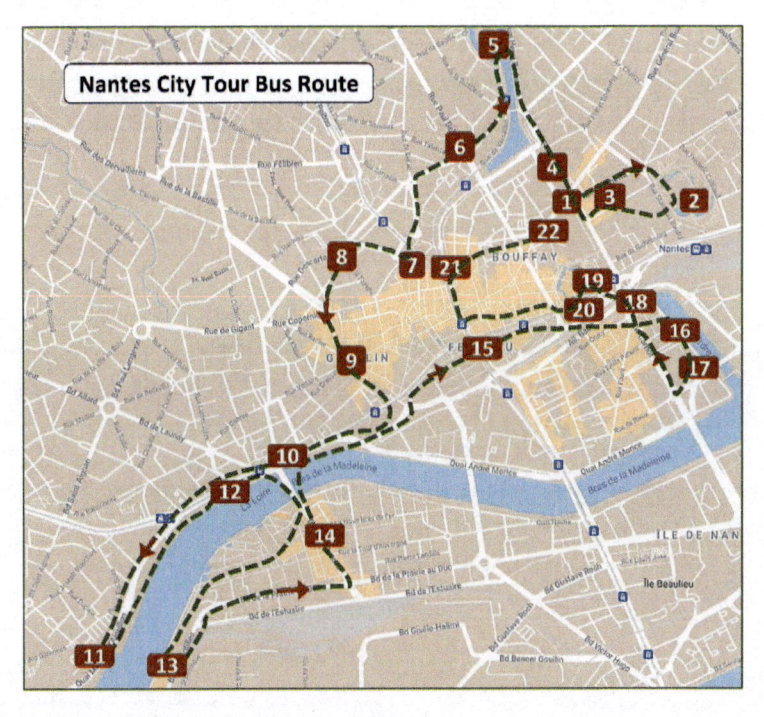

Nantes City Tour Bus Route

Website: Full details may be found at: **CityTour-Nantes.fr.** Reservations and ticket purchase may be made on this site.

Tickets: Tickets may be purchased via the Nantes Tourist Office website **(www.Nantes-Tourisme.com)** or from many third-party agencies such as Trip Advisor.

Nantes Pass: This ride is free to holders of the Nantes Pass.

Availability & Frequency: The availability of this service varies by the season and, in in recent months, the COVID health emergency has negatively impacted the number of trips available. During high season from April through September, this bus tour generally runs 4 times per day. Due to the varying availability, it is suggested you visit the agency's website before making final plans.

Price: Adults: 12€ / Children 5-12 6€ / Children under 5 are free.

Starting Point: Nantes Tourist Office near the Château des ducs. 9 Rue des États, Nantes.

Points Along the Route: See map on previous page. In addition, the following chapter provides details on many of these attractions.

1. Place Foch – historical plaza
2. Jardin de Plantes – botanical garden
3. Musée des Arts – Nantes art museum
4. Cours Saint André – broad, attractive street
5. Ile de Versailles – Japanese Zen Garden along the River Erdre
6. Talensac – open market
7. Tour Bretagne – tall building with rooftop overlook
8. Place Aristide Briand – square in the center of town
9. Place Graslin – popular square in the heart of old town
10. Quai de la Fosse – Loire riverfront district
11. Musée Jules Verne – Jules Verne Museum

Getting Around Nantes

12. Musée Naval – Naval destroyer open for tours
13. Les Anneaux du Hangar – popular walkway and park on the Île de Nantes.
14. Les Machines de Île – large, mobile machines in a Jules Verne theme.
15. Ile Feydeu – historical neighborhood which was once an island.
16. Canal St Félix – marina and canal which runs under the city.
17. Cité des Congrés – Large concert and convention center along the River Erdre
18. Tour LU – historical building in Centre Ville
19. Château des ducs – large castle and museum
20. Miroir d'Eau – water mirror next to the Château des Ducs
21. Cours des 50 Otages – a main street in central Nantes
22. Cathédrale St. Pierre & St. Paul – large cathedral

Bicycle Rentals:

A Bicloo Bike Rental Station.
Photo Source: Google Maps

A Starting-Point Guide

Nantes is an easy city and area to explore by bicycle. There are over 230 miles (around 370 kilometers) of cycle routes in the

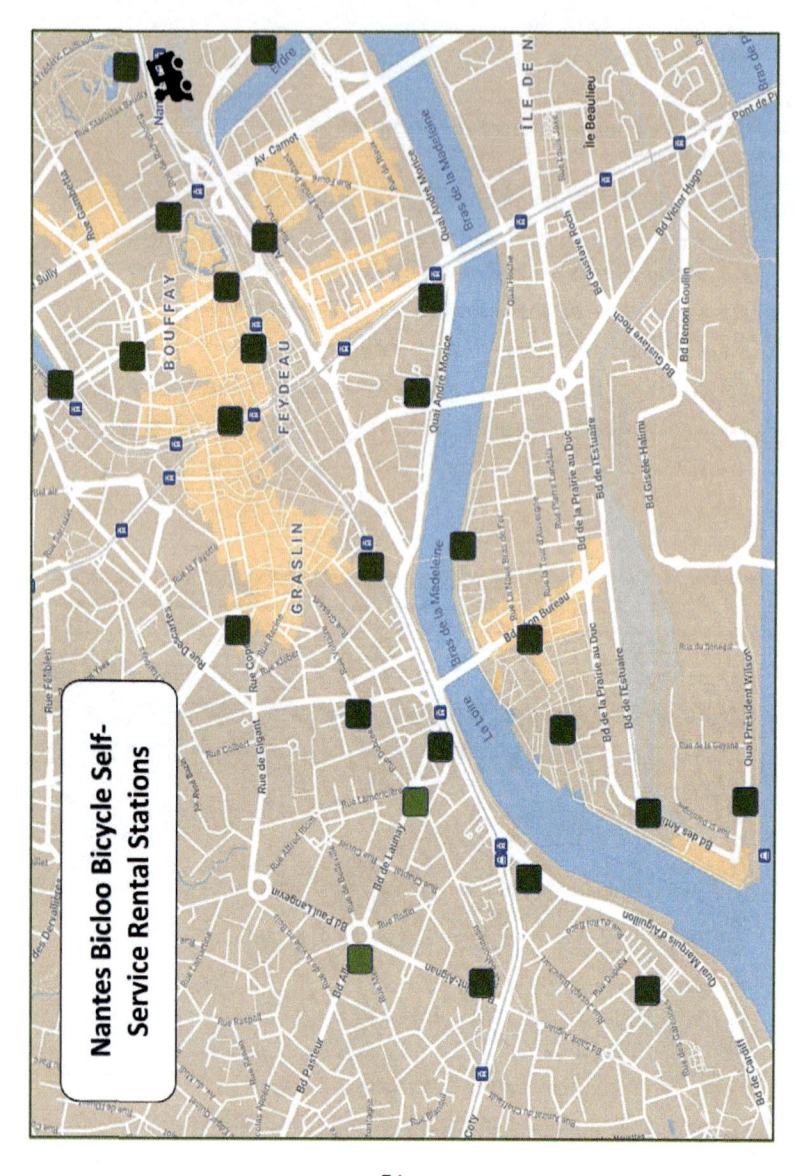

Nantes Bicloo Bicycle Self-Service Rental Stations

Getting Around Nantes

city area. In addition, there are many enjoyable routes out of the city such as a ride to the coast or east to wine country.

In Nantes, there are several bicycle rental agencies. The most popular service is **Bicloo.** This is a bicycle sharing service with over 1,000 bicycles at more than one-hundred pick-up/drop-off spots.

Not every station is guaranteed to have bicycles available. It is suggested you download the **Bicloo app** which will indicate which stations have available bikes when you are looking to use one.

Bike stands are self-service. You simply need to use a credit card (or set up an account in the app) to unlock a bike and the charge will be applied up to the point when the bicycle is returned. You may return a bike to any stand which has an open position.

Cost for Bicycle Rental: (As of mid-2022) The Bicloo website, listed below, cites several different rate options, and you may establish a plan on the site.

- First 30-minutes are free
- Rates increase with duration of usage. After the free 30-minutes, there is a fee of 0,50€ for the next 30-minutes, then of €1,00 followed by an additional of 2€ for subsequent 30-minute periods. Example Total Fares:
- 1-Hour or less = 0,50€
- 2 Hours = 3,50€

Nantes Pass: Includes one day free bicycle rental per pass holder.

Website: **www.Bicloo.NantesMetropole.fr.**

~ ~ ~ ~ ~ ~

7: Central Nantes Attractions

Nante's main attractions are primarily in or close to the historical center, often referred to as Old Town. Many of the sights are within walking distance of the center of town while some, such as the Jules Verne Museum and those on the Île de Nantes, are best reached by using the local transportation network.

There is a good variety of sights in Nantes which include traditional yet impressive museums. There are also several places which will provide experiences unique to Nantes and the region such as the popular "Les Machines de I'île." This has several huge fantastical rides crafted in the style of Jules Verne.

For food lovers, there is an expansive open market, the Talensac Market, with numerous stands of local seafood, food, and wines.

This chapter outlines the more popular attractions and locations near the center of town. The next chapter details the most popular sights on the edge of town. Each of this second group will require either driving to them or taking local transportation.

One caution, not all sights are open during the same days and hours. Details on opening hours are included in the attraction descriptions which follow.

The map on the next page indicates where each of these attractions may be found.

Nantes Points of Interest

Attractions In Central Nantes

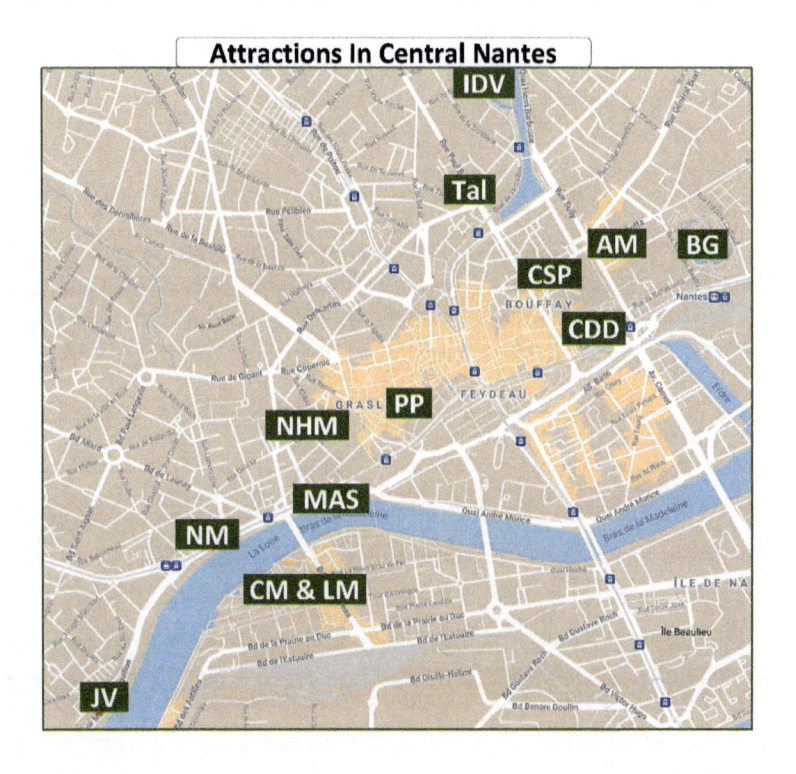

Nantes Attractions Map Legend	
Map Code	Attraction
AM	Arts Museum
BG	Botanical Garden
CDD	Château des ducs de Bretagne & History Museum
CSP	Cathedral of St. Peter and St. Paul

Nantes Attractions Map Legend	
Map Code	Attraction
IDV	île de Versailles
JV	Jules Verne Museum
LM & CM	Les Machines & Carousel of the Marine Worlds
MAS	Memorial to the Abolition of Slavery
NHM	Natural History Museum
NM	Naval Museum
PP	Passage Pommeraye
Tal	Talensac Market

Arts Museum / Musée D' Arts de Nantes:

An impressive art museum with a comprehensive collection with over 12,000 items covering nine centuries of art.

The museum was extensively renovated in 2017 giving it a fresh feel. Visitors will find art works from such notables as Picasso, Monet, Courbet, and others. Plan on a visit of two or more hours to discover the highlights.

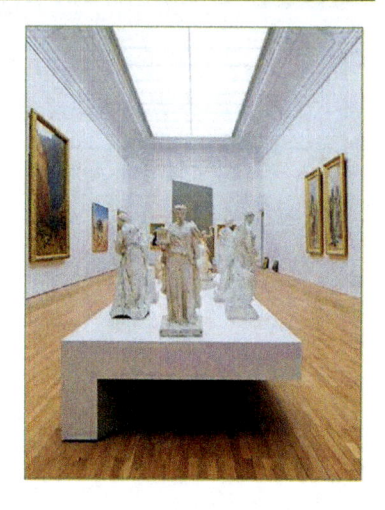

Art Museum Details[7]	
Location:	10 Rue Georges Clemenceau 44000 Nantes
Entrance Fee:	8€ Adult. Free for under 18
Included in Pass Nantes:	Yes. No fee for Pass Nantes holders
Tram and Bus Stops Nearby:	Tram: none Bus: Lines 11 & 12
Facilities:	Restaurant and bathrooms Museum shop & bookstore
Hours:	Closed Tuesday Summer: 10am to 7pm Fall-Winter-Spring: 11am to 7pm
Nearby:	1 block from the botanical garden. No shops or restaurants in the immediate vicinity of the museum.
Website:	**MuseeDArts-deNantes.NantesMetropole.fr** (no dash after "Arts")

---

[7] **COVID Note**: Most museums in Nantes and all of France require a current COVID vaccination certificate to enter. Rules around this do change frequently.

Botanical Garden / Jardin des Plantes:

An inviting and well-developed park in the heart of Nantes. This is a perfect place to step away from city traffic and noise. The gardens cover 17 acres in a pleasant mix of walking paths, formal gardens, ponds, and open spaces. It is considered to be one of the top botanical gardens in France.

More than 10,000 plant species may be found here and each year over 5,000 flowering plants are on display across the open gardens and greenhouses. Camelias are a specialty, and many are on display. In addition to plant life, several notable sculptures and fountains are on the grounds including one honoring Jules Verne.

Plan on taking at least an hour to wander through the open areas and greenhouses. A tearoom and terrace for dining are open most of the year.

The Nantes Botanical Garden has several trails, ponds, and gardens to explore.
A relaxing retreat in the heart of the city.

Botanical Garden Details	
Entrance Fee:	No fee to visit the open gardens and most greenhouses. Extra fees apply for taking a guided greenhouse tour.
Train Stop Nearby:	The southern entrance to the park is across from the train station and tram line 1. Note, this entrance is at the far side of the park from the tearoom and greenhouses.
Facilities:	Tea room, Merry-Go-Round, and restrooms.
Hours:	Hours are seasonal. The park is open every day, but greenhouse tours are limited. Check website for tour availability for the dates you will be in Nantes. Summer: 8:30am to 8pm Spring & Fall: 8:30am to 6:30pm Winter: 8:30am to 5:30pm
Nearby:	Several restaurants are at the southern entrance near the train station.
Website:	**Jardins.Nantes.fr** – then navigate to details on the botanical garden.

Château des ducs de Bretagne & History Museum:

Often referred to as the "Nantes Castle," this complex is the most iconic in this city. The former castle of the Dukes of Brittany was built primarily in the 15th century as the ducal palace for all of the Brittany region. It was started by the Dukes of Brittany in the 13th century as a defensive fortress along the river and over time was added on to and improved.

Château des ducs de Bretagne
Fortress and history museum

At varying times during its history, this set of buildings served as a fortress, a palace, and even a prison. It is an impressive complex with ramparts (fortified walls) and a moat surrounding the structure. Visitors may roam the interior courtyard and the ramparts freely.

There is a restaurant and gift shop here. In good weather, you may dine outdoors on the grounds.

Within the Château, is an impressive history museum which is sometimes referred to as the "**Nantes Urban History Museum**." Given all of the history this fortress/château has seen, this is a perfect spot to highlight the history of the city, building, and area. This is a large museum with over 30 rooms of exhibits including several interactive exhibits.

Plan on a minimum of 2 hours to tour both the Chateau and museum.

Château des ducs & History Museum Details	
Location:	4 Place Marc Elder 44000 Nantes
Entrance Fee:	Varies by what you will visit: No charge to visit the courtyard, ramparts, and gardens. There is a fee to visit the museum and other temporary exhibits. Adult 8€ and 5€ for individuals 18-25. Children are free.
Included in Pass Nantes:	Yes. No entrance fee to the history museum for Pass Nantes holders
Tram and Bus Stops Nearby:	Tram: Line 1 – Duchesse Anne stop Bus: Lines 4 Also – this is just a 10-minute walk from the Nantes train station.
Facilities:	Restaurant, bookshop, and bathrooms. Picnic area in the castle grounds.
Hours:	Open every day. Fall-Winter-Spring 8:30am to 7pm Summer: 8:30am to 8pm

Château des ducs & History Museum Details	
Nearby:	The Miroir d'eau (a large reflecting pool) is across the street, (CR Franklin Roosevelt.) There are a few restaurants and shops along the northern and western walk around the Château. A parking lot is along the eastern side. Caution, in high season, this fills up quickly.
Website:	**ChateauNantes.fr**

There are over 20 rooms of exhibits on several floors within the history museum situated inside the Château des ducs de Bretagne.

~ ~ ~ ~ ~ ~

Cathedral of St. Peter & St. Paul of Nantes / Nantes Cathedral:

Located near the Château des ducs is the impressive Nantes Cathedral (Cathedral of St. Peter and St. Paul of Nantes). This Roman Catholic church stands 192 feet tall and towers over much of the historical area. Construction of this Gothic style church took over 450 years, starting in early 15th century and not completed until late in the 19th century.

The Cathedral of St. Peter and St. Paul of Nantes

In very recent times, 2020, a fire broke out inside the cathedral damaging three areas. The main organ built in 1621 was destroyed as a result. The cathedral is closed for restoration and, as of this writing, has not fully reopened.

At the front entrance to the cathedral is Place Saint-Pierre, an attractive open square with several restaurants and shops. This square is also the location where several tours of Nantes start.

Cathedral of St. Peter and St. Paul Details	
Location:	7 Imp. Saint-Laurent 44000 Nantes
Entrance Fee:	No entrance fee
Tram and Bus Stops Nearby:	No tram lines stop here. The closest line #1 is a 2-block walk away. Numerous bus lines stop near here including lines 11, 12, & 348.
Hours:	Closed due to restoration. Check the website for updates.
Nearby:	Les Cryptes – Underground crypts and museum adjacent to the cathedral. Major attractions including the Arts Museum and the Château des ducs are less than a 5-minute walk. Numerous restaurants are near the cathedral.
Website:	**Cathedrale-Nantes.fr**

~ ~ ~ ~ ~ ~

Île de Versailles / Island of Versailles:

A short distance north of the center of Nantes is a small manmade island in the middle of the Erdre River. The island contains a collection of Asian and European plants and trees. The draw here is not only to view an ornate garden, but to find a quiet and attractive spot to stroll and relax such as spending time in the Zen Garden.

The Japanese Gardens on the Île de Versailles.

Visitors to this island may enjoy a light meal in the Tea Room in the the Maison de l'Erdre, or rent canoes, kayaks, and small boats to explore the river. Though the island was given the name "Versailles," it does not relate to the noted palace of Versailles near Paris.

Île de Versailles Details	
Location:	Quai de Versailles 44000 Nantes
Entrance Fee:	No fee to enter.
Tram and Bus Stops Nearby:	Tram: Line 2 -- Saint-Mihiel stop. Then walk 1 block north to a bridge which takes you onto the island.
Facilities:	A Japanese tea house is located at the northern end of the island. Public restrooms. Canoe and boat rentals.
Hours:	Hours can vary by the season and day. Closed on Thursdays. General hours are: 8:30am to 8pm from March to October.
Nearby:	Several restaurants, including floating restaurants, may be found just south of the park near the tram stop. A Bicloo bicycle station is at the southern entrance to the park.
Website:	Jardins.Nantes.fr - then navigate to the page titled "Garden of the Island of Versailles"

~ ~ ~ ~ ~ ~

Nantes Points of Interest

Jules Verne Museum:

A short distance southwest from central Nantes is a museum dedicated to the famed writer Jules Verne (Musée Jules Verne). The fairly small museum sits on a bluff overlooking the Loire River. Jules Verne did not live in this building, but the location was selected as it is similar to the atmosphere which guided much of his writings.

The Jules Verne Museum
Photo Source: Wikimedia - by Pasdenom

This museum is located on several floors and there are eight different rooms with memorabilia from his early life and several models inspired by his work. Touring the museum generally will take about one hour or less.

Jules Verne Museum Details	
Location:	3 Rue de l'Hermitage 44000 Nantes
Entrance Fee:	Adults = 3€

Jules Verne Museum Details	
	Children = 1,50€
Included in Pass Nantes:	Yes. No entrance fee to the Jules Verne Museum for Pass Nantes holders
Tram and Bus Stops Nearby:	Trams do not come near here. The closest tram stop, Gare Maritime is a 10-minute walk. To travel by bus, take line C-1 to Le Chat. From there, it is an 8-minute walk.
Facilities:	Restrooms and a small shop. Elevators are available for individuals with limited mobility.
Hours:	Closed on Tuesday. Open Saturday from 10am to 6pm with a 2-hour closure for lunch. All other days the museum is open from 2pm to 6pm.
Nearby:	The Nantes Planetarium is just one block from here. Avenue Sainte-Anne next to the museum is a pleasant stroll with several small shops and restaurants. The Maritime Museum is a 10-minute walk toward the center of town and is also a good spot to catch a tram.
Website:	**JulesVerne.NantesMetropole.fr**

Nantes Points of Interest

Les Machines & Carousel of the Marine Worlds:

The island of Île de Nantes, which sits in the middle of the Loire River, hosts a unique set of attractions unlike any found elsewhere. Modeled in part after Jules Verne, the Les Machines de Lîle (The Machines of the Isle of Nantes) was launched to help promote Nantes as a city of creativity.

Les Machines de Lîle
"Le Grand Elephant" and "Sea Worlds Carousel"
Photo Source: LesMachines-Nantes.fr

Plan on spending several hours here as there are multiple components to "Les Machines" including:

La Galerie des Machines / the Gallery of Machines. Come to view and even ride a large variety of fantastical mechanical creatures. There is also the gallery laboratory where you may watch new creatures being built.

Le Grand Elephant. A large mechanical elephant which will take you and others for a ride around a portion of the island.

A Starting-Point Guide

Carrousel des Mondes Marins / Carousel of the Marine Worlds. A multi-level merry-go-round with a variety of machines and creatures to ride and control.

	Les Machines & Carousel Details
Location:	On the Île de Nantes Parc des Chantiers Bd Léon Bureau 44200 Nantes
Entrance Fee:	Varies by what you will visit or ride: Each of three attractions: Big Elephant, the Machine Gallery or the Carousel costs: Adult = 8,50€, Child = 6,90€ per attraction.
Included in Pass Nantes:	Choice of the Gallery or the Carousel is included in the Nantes Pass. Discounted rates for visiting both.
Tram and Bus Stops Nearby:	Not adjacent to any tram stop. Tram: Line 1 stop "Chantiers Navals" is less than a 10-minute walk across the Loire. Bus line 5 stop Prairie au Duc is close to Les Machines.
Facilities:	Restaurant, gift shop, and bathrooms.
Hours:	Closed January. Feb and March – 2pm to 6pm All other month's hours may vary by day, but generally is open from 10am to 6pm – occasionally later.

Nantes Points of Interest

Les Machines & Carousel Details	
Nearby:	Les Annex de Burean – also referred to as "The Rings."
Website:	**LesMachines-Nantes.fr**

Memorial to the Abolition of Slavery:

One of the world's largest monuments to slavery and its elimination may be found in Nantes along the Loire River. This is a somber but important acknowledgement of Nante's role in slavery.

The Memorial to the Abolition of Slavery
"Mémorial de L'abolition de L'esclavage"

The entire exhibit is below street level. Visitors encounter a lengthy passage with many narrow chambers. Among the features are details on the slave ships which departed from Nantes for America.

Memorial to the Abolition of Slavery Details	
Location:	Quai de la Fosse 44000 Nantes Along the Loire River adjacent to the Pont Anne de Bretagne (bridge)
Entrance Fee:	There is no entrance fee to view this memorial.
Tram and Bus Stops Nearby:	Tram line #1 – Chantiers Navals stop. Bus line 11 – Chantiers Navals stop.
Facilities:	There are no shops, restaurants, or bathrooms at the memorial.
Hours:	Open every day. Fall and Winter hours are 9am to 6pm. Spring and Summer hours are 9am to 8pm.
Nearby:	The Naval Museum is a short walk from here. River cruises dock is quite close. Many Loire River cruises start or end from this location.
Website:	**Memorial.Nantes.fr**

Natural History Museum:

Nantes Natural History Museum
Photo Source: Wikimedia by Francois de Dijon

The "Muséum d'Histoire Naturelle de Nantes" is considered one of France's premier museums devoted to zoology, wildlife, and minerology. The museum was established in the 1800s and now has a rich collection spread across two floors. One of the more popular exhibits is a full skeleton of a whale.

Plan on spending at least two hours here to view the main exhibits.

Natural History Museum Details	
Location:	12 Rue Voltaire 44000 Nantes A short walk west from Place Graslin
Entrance Fee:	Adults: 4€ Children: 2€

Natural History Museum Details	
Included in Pass Nantes:	Yes. No entrance fee to this museum for Pass Nantes holders
Tram and Bus Stops Nearby:	No tram lines stop near here. The closest bus stops are along Rue Copernic, a short walk north from the museum.
Facilities:	Restrooms, elevator. Small amount of gift items at the reception desk.
Hours:	Closed on Tuesday Most other days: 10am to 6pm
Nearby:	Place Graslin is a 3-minute walk from here. Several restaurants and shops are on Rue Voltaire, the avenue facing the main museum entrance.
Website:	**Museum.NantesMetropole.fr**

~ ~ ~ ~ ~ ~

Naval Museum:

Naval Museum
French Destroyer "Maillé Brézé"
Photo Source: Google Earth

The Musée Naval Maillé Bréze is France's first floating naval museum. This is a retired destroyer built in 1950 which, when active, had a crew of 277 officers and men.

To visit this interesting monument to France's maritime history you must join a guided tour. Overall time to visit and tour the ship will typically be under one hour.

Naval Museum Details	
Location:	Quay at the Pit 44000 Nantes (On the banks of the Loire)
Entrance Fee:	Adults 10€

Naval Museum Details	
	Children 6€
Included in Pass Nantes:	Yes. No entrance fee to the Naval Museum for Pass Nantes holders
Tram and Bus Stops Nearby:	Tram: Line 1 – Gare Maritime is very close to the Naval Museum.
Facilities:	Restrooms. There is no restaurant here.
Hours:	Visits are limited to guided tours at set times and most tours are held only in the afternoon at 30-minute intervals with the first tour starting at 2:30pm. Check website for current schedule.
Nearby:	The Jules Verne Museum is a 10-minute walk. Memorial to the Abolition of Slavery is a short, pleasant walk along the Loire. There is little in the way of restaurants or shops near here.
Website:	**MailleBreze.com**

~ ~ ~ ~ ~ ~

Passage Pommeraye:

In central Nantes is an ornate shopping mall which was first opened in 1843. While this shopping center is small when measured against current standards, what makes it special is the era of this mall and the Renaissance-era statues, grand staircase, and décor. Coming here gives the visitor the feel of wandering through an ornate museum.

Passage Pommeraye - Historic Shopping Mall
Photo Source: Wikimedia - by Velvet

Passage Pommeraye Details	
Location:	Rue de la Fosse 44000 Nantes Midway between Place Royale and Place Graslin

Passage Pommeraye Details	
Entrance Fee:	No fee to enter and explore this shopping center.
Tram and Bus Stops Nearby:	The closest tram stop is the "Commerce" tram stop which services all three tram lines. From this stop it is a 7- or 8-minute walk.
Hours:	Open every day until 8pm. Opening time is 8am on weekdays and 9am on weekends.
Nearby:	The Passage Pommeraye is in the heart of the main shopping area for Nantes. Near here are the historical Place Royale and Place Graslin.
Website:	**PassagePommeraye.fr**

~ ~ ~ ~ ~ ~

Talensac Market:

The "Marché de Talensac" is a large food market which has been active for nearly 80 years. It is a great place to explore the region's cuisine including fish, produce, baked goods, and meats.

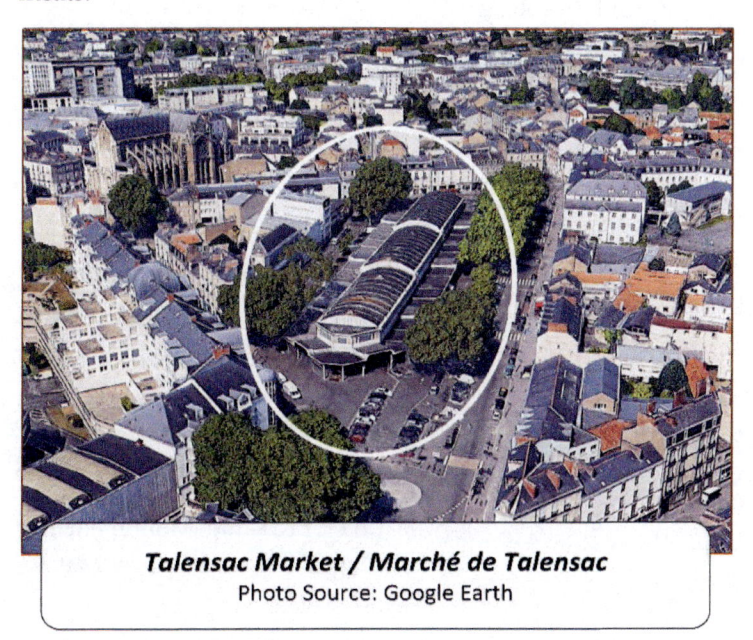

Talensac Market / Marché de Talensac
Photo Source: Google Earth

There are several booths selling light meals, so consider taking some time to sit and have a snack while here. The market is slightly out of the way of the primary historic center, but worth the trip if you enjoy discovering local products.

Talensac Market / Marché de Talensac Details	
Location:	Rue Talensac
	44000 Nantes

Talensac Market / Marché de Talensac Details	
Entrance Fee:	There is no fee to enter this market.
Tram and Bus Stops Nearby:	Tram: Line 2 – 50 Otages stops 1 block from Talensac. Bus: Lines 12 and 23 stop at Talensac.
Facilities:	Restroom. Some eating areas adjoining several food stalls.
Hours:	Varies by the day – and, when open, it is just in the mornings and early afternoon. Monday – closed unless it is a public holiday. Weekends – 8am to 1:30pm Tues to Fri – 8am to 1pm
Nearby:	The River Erde and Monument to 50 hostages is close to this market. The Île de Versailles and its Japanese garden is a 10-minute walk. Numerous cafes and restaurants are in the area.
Website:	Marche-Talensac.fr

~ ~ ~ ~ ~ ~

8: Attractions on the Edge of Nantes

In addition to the major attractions in or near the historical center of Nantes, there are several sights to consider just on the outskirts of town. These can create a broader understanding of this area and culture.

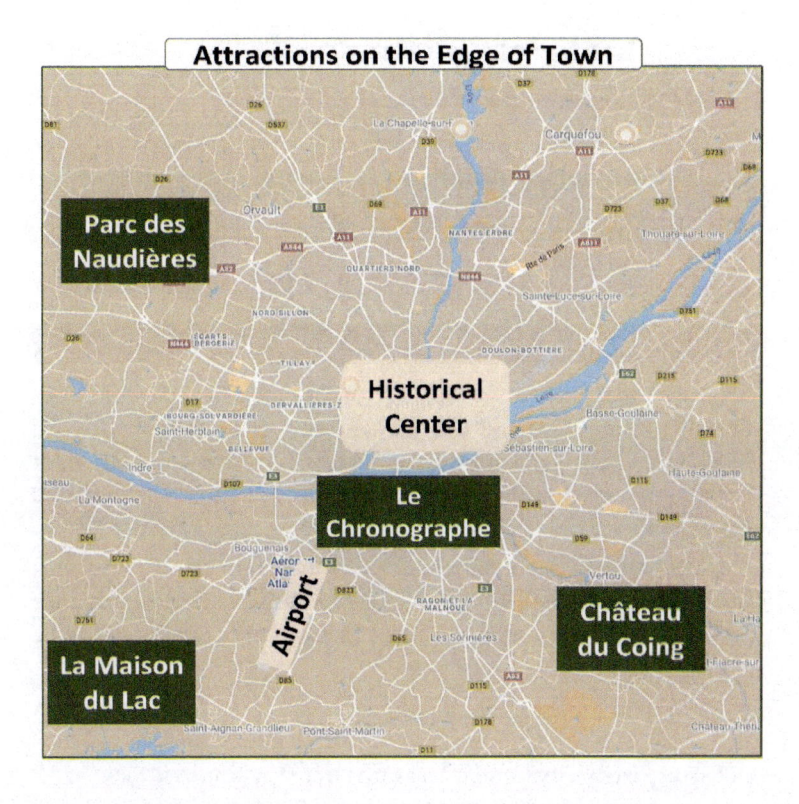

Attractions on the Edge of Town

There is something in these attractions for everyone ranging from relaxing parks to wine tasting, and even amusement parks. None of these locales are reachable by the tram system, but several may be reached by local buses.

| Attractions on the Edge of Nantes ||||
Name	Type	Distance from City Center [8]	Accessible by Train or bus
Château du Coing	Vineyard with Tastings	17 km	No
La Maison du Lac	Museum & Nature Center	19 km	No
Le Chronographe	Archeological Museum	6 km	Yes
Parc des Naudières	Amusement Park	21 km	Yes

Château du Coing / Quince Castle:

A visit to this lovely chateau provides an enjoyable combination of a visit to a small historic castle and a tour with tastings of local wine. This is a family vineyard focusing on Muscadet wines – the area associated with the western end of the Loire River Valley.

The chateau dates back as far as the 16th century and was fully restored in the 19th century. Tours are provided by advance reservation. In addition to local tours, the complex offers bicycle,

---

[8] **Distance from City Center:** Measured from Château des ducs.

canoe, and Segway rentals to provide fun alternatives to explore the expansive grounds.

For food lovers, a special treat are the food and wine paring events which take place in the evenings on limited occasions.

For all visits, tours, rentals, and events, it is important to check the website first to ensure availability and, when appropriate, make reservations.

Château du Coing Details	
Location:	Château du Coing 44690 Saint-Fiacre-sur-Maine
Traveling to the Chateau:	Cars are a must. There are no convenient bus stops close to this complex. Driving is a 25-to-30-minute trip each way.
Facilities:	Tasting room with small shop and bathrooms.
Hours:	Hours vary by the season. Closed on Sundays and holidays. Typical hours are split with open late morning, closed for lunch, and open again for a couple hours in the afternoon.
Nearby:	Several other wine chateaux with tasting rooms are in the vicinity. All require driving to them.
Website:	**vgc.fr**

La Maison du Lac:

The "La Maison du Lac de Grand-Lieu" is an expansive ecological park located next to Lake Grand-Lieu, France's oldest lake. This preserve is a large bird sanctuary of over 10,000 acres. Access to the lake and natural preserve is restricted, so a visit to La Maison du Lac with its approved trails is a great way to experience this element of nature.

The chateau, which is the starting point for adventures here, was the former hunting lodge of Jean-Pierre Guerlain, a noted French perfumer. A visit here has several components including an interactive exposition center, nature walks and even workshops on photography and the local ecosystem.

Advance reservations are advised, and tickets should be purchased via the website. Allow for a minimum of a 2-hour visit if you wish to do the nature walk while here.

	La Maison du Lac Details
Location:	Rue du lac 44830, Bouaye
Entrance Fee:	Separate fees for visiting the Exhibition Center or taking the Environmental Walk. The best rate is to purchase the package which includes all components. Adults: 8€ or under 18 = 5€
Included in Pass Nantes:	Not included
Tram and Bus Stops Nearby:	Cars are needed. There are no convenient train or bus stops close by.

La Maison du Lac Details

Facilities:	Gift shop and bathrooms.
Hours:	Hours vary by the season with winter having the most limited open times. Typically closed on Monday. During high season the hours will typically range from 10am to 6:30pm.
Nearby:	The neighboring villages of Bouaye and Passay offer a good variety of services. While in Passay, stop in to "The Fishermen's House" for a different view of the lake.
Website:	MaisonDuLacGrandLieu.com

Le Chronographe:

The remnants of the ancient Roman community Ratiatum were found under a farm field behind a church in the village Rezé. An archeological project was initiated in the 1980's.

Today, in addition to this being an

ongoing archeology program, visitors may view many of the items found and tour the site to learn the history of this site. For children, there are several interactive exhibits which help them learn about the science of archeology and what life was like here so long ago.

When visiting, plan on a visit of roughly one hour. There is no food service available here.

Le Chronographe Details	
Location:	21 rue de Saint Lupien 44000 Reze In the village of Rezé, immediately south of Nantes.
Entrance Fee	Adult 3€ Under 25 1,50€
Included in Pass Nantes:	Yes – free admission.
Train or Bus Stop Nearby:	No close tram stop Bus lines 30 and 97 stop at "Le Corbusier" which is only 1 block from Le Chronographe.
Hours:	Closed Monday all year. Closed Tuesday Sept-to June Opening hours are 2pm to 6pm.
Nearby:	Minimal. There is very little around the Chronographe to visit or tour.
Website:	leChronographe.NantesMetropole.fr

Attractions on the Edge of Town

Parc des Naudières:

A short drive northwest from Nantes is a mid-size amusement park which can be a delight for children, especially in the summer months. The Naudières Park or "Parc des Naudières" offers visitors a mix of entertainment including rides, a beach park, go-cart track, and even boat rides on the park's lake.

This is not a large park, but the designers have packed in a good variety of activities geared to children and families.

Parc des Naudières Details	
Location:	1 Les Naudières 44880 Sautron In the village of Sautron, a half-hour drive northwest from the center of Nantes.
Entrance Fee	Adult 17€ Children 11€ Seniors 13€
Included in Pass Nantes:	No
Train or Bus Stop Nearby:	No close tram stop Bus line 320 stops outside of the entrance to this amusement park.
Facilities:	Restrooms. Snack bars and restaurant.

Parc des Naudières Details	
Hours:	Closed October thru March Limited hours and days for April, May, and September. In September, the park is only open on weekends. In high season of July and August, the park is open from 10am to 7pm.
Nearby:	This park is on the outskirts of town with few stores or restaurants nearby. A go-cart park is very close "City Kart."
Website:	**LesNaudieres.com**

~ ~ ~ ~ ~ ~

9: Coastal Towns to Explore

One of the great aspects of Nantes is the proximity to the coast and its many beaches, towns, and villages. Luckily, if you do not have a car, many of these delightful destinations may be reached by train. It is easy to have a relaxing day trip from Nantes to the beach or stroll through oceanfront boardwalks with shops and cafes.

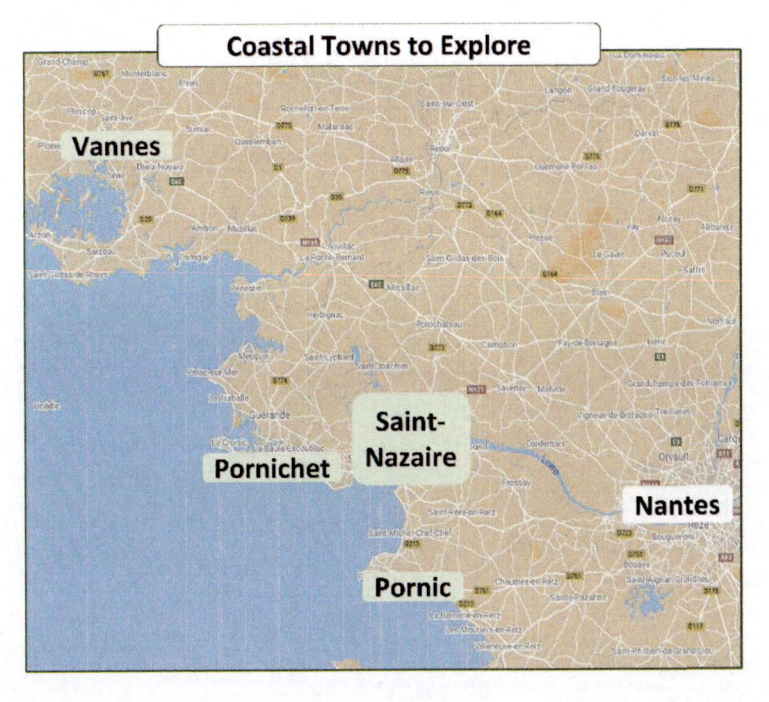

A Starting-Point Guide

This is a very popular region for vacationers from central France looking to escape from the city and it is also a noted destination for individuals from the U.K. The beach areas and beautiful rocky shorelines are dotted with numerous small inns, camping sites, and beachfront homes. Taking a drive along the beach, especially in the summer and fall, is an enjoyable experience.

This area is more than beaches and tourist-friendly towns. Given the settlements at different times by the Celtic, Romans, and Britons, an interesting mix of history and structures may be found here. Several of the towns have impressive sights to visit such as the fortified city walls in Vannes.

Listed in this chapter are four of the many popular coastal towns. In each case, they are within easy reach of Nantes by train or car. Not every town described has beach access, but most do.

Suggested Coastal Towns to Visit from Nantes

Town	Population	Coast or Beach Access?	Drive Time from central Nantes	Travel Time by Train
Pornic	15,000	Yes	45min	1hr
Pornichet	11,000	Yes	55min	50 min
Saint-Nazaire	70,000	Yes	50min	40 min
Vannes	53,000	No	1hr 15min+	1hr 30min

Coastal Towns to Explore

Pornic:

Pornic is an ideal small harbor town. If you are taking the train, it lets you off right next to the harbor, so your adventure can begin immediately. This is a relaxing town to explore along the quai and watch the boats come and go as you visit the many shops and outdoor restaurants.

The center of town is set back along a harbor and not right on the ocean. To reach most of the beaches, a drive or bike ride will be required. There are many beaches along the 15km stretch known as the "Coastal Road."

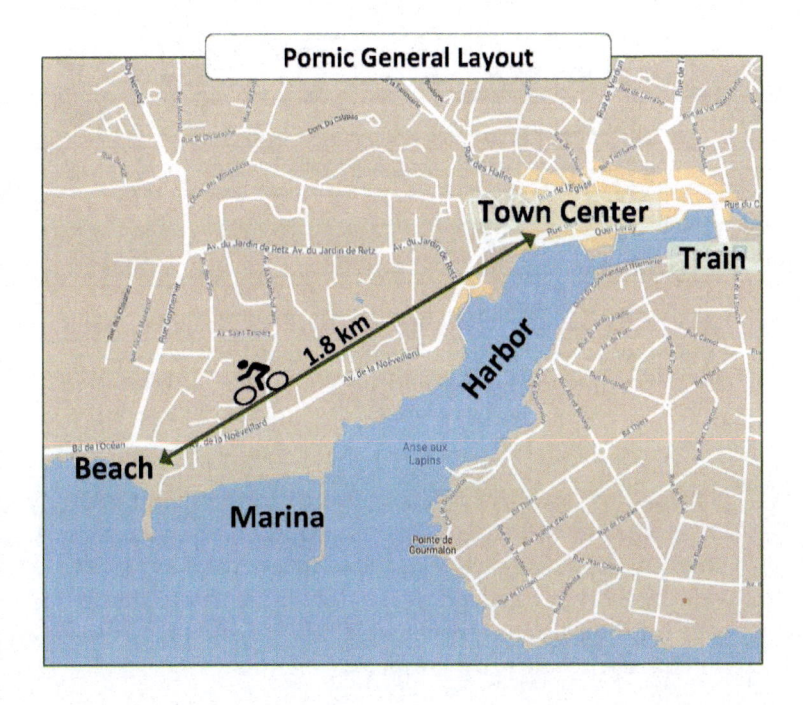

Pornic General Layout

Map showing Town Center, Train, Harbor, Beach, and Marina, with a 1.8 km bike route from Beach to Town Center.

The Pornic harbor area is a pleasure to explore.
Photo Source: Daniel Jolivet - Wikimedia Commons

Pornic Highlights:

- Tourist Office: The Pornic tourist information center "Intercommunal Tourist Office of Pornic" is next to the train station. First-time visitors should stop in to chat with the staff as they can provide detailed maps on the town, best sightseeing spots, beaches, and other sights. **En.Pornic.com**

- Château de Pornic: A castle and former fortress built in the 10th century by the Duke of Brittany. The castle and gardens, which overlook the harbor, are close to town and are easy to walk to. This is a private residence, so visits are limited. Tours of the gardens are available. More details are available at: **www.ChateauDe Pornic.fr**.

- Beaches: Several beaches and beach parks are near Pornic. This is where the map and information from the tourist information center can come in handy to help locate a beach which fits your preferences. The closest beach, Plage de la Noëveillard, is next to the marina and is an easy bike ride from the heart of town.

> **Rent an e-bike while in Pornic for easy access to the beaches. The rental shop for "Sea Bike & Sun" is close to the train station.**

- Little Tourist Train: During the summer, an open-air train takes visitors on a 40-minute tour of the area.

- Markets: If you are lucky to be in town on a market day, normally Wednesday through Sunday, it is worth checking out. Seafood, especially mussels and clams, are specialties of the area.

Traveling to Pornic:

- Train: A train trip from Nantes takes approximately 1 hour. The train station in Pornic is very close to the harbor and center of town. There are a limited number of trains each day, so take care to check the schedule. Trains make numerous stops along this scenic route.

  Once you arrive in Pornic, and if you want to explore the beaches or area outside of the town, consider renting an e-bike. The firm "Sea Bike and Sun" is very close to the train station and near the tourist office.

- Driving: A drive from central Nantes takes around 45 to 50 minutes. If you take the most direct route, it is largely through open farming lands with several villages along the way. Parking lots in Pornic are along the harbor and marina. During high season these lots can fill up early.

A Starting-Point Guide

Pornichet:

The area known as "Cote d'Amour" is a beach lover's dream. There are many miles of beaches here and the attractive tourist town of Pornichet is a great place to start explorations.

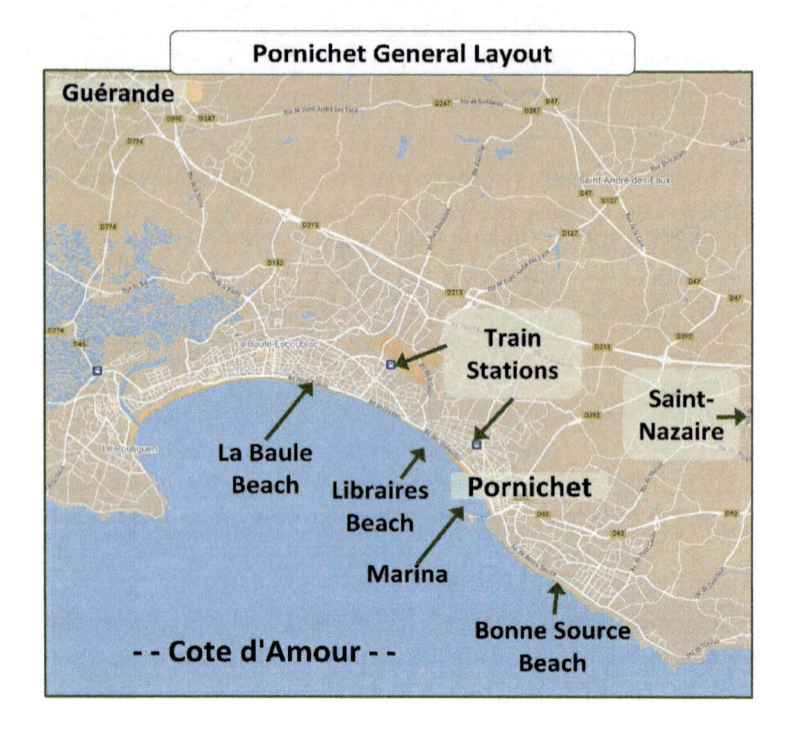

Pornichet General Layout

- Guérande
- Train Stations
- Saint-Nazaire
- La Baule Beach
- Libraires Beach
- Pornichet
- Marina
- Bonne Source Beach
- - - Cote d'Amour - -

This is a town and area fully dedicated to tourism. In addition to the long beach walks, there are casinos, numerous hotels, and apartments for rent. There is also a seemingly endless array of cafes and dining options. Given the gentle climate and beautiful stretches of beaches, it is a popular spot for French, British, and other Europeans to vacation. Be prepared to encounter crowds during the summer months.

This town is easy to visit from Nantes for a day trip or, as many people do, consider spending your full vacation time here.

The beaches near Pornichet stretch for several miles.
Photo Source: Google Earth

The beaches are not all within easy walking distance of central Pornichet or its twin neighboring town of La Baule-Les-Pins. In some cases, beaches such as Bonne Source, which sits slightly south of Pornichet and its marina, will require local transportation or use of a rental bicycle. Most bicycle rental services include E-bikes as an option which allow for a more relaxing ride.

Pornichet Highlights:

- Tourist Office: The Pornichet tourist office, "Office de Tourisme de Pornichet," is conveniently located near the marina and close to beaches. Pick up a detailed area map, obtain information on vacation rentals, and even book tours. Full details may be found at: **www.Pornichet.fr**.
- Beaches: There are several kilometers of family-friendly beaches which are great for sunbathing, relaxing on the sand, or enjoying water sports. The beaches and beach parks

within walking or bicycle distance include, but not limited to, Bonne-Source, Libraires Beach, and La Baule Beach.
- Hippodrome: If you enjoy horse racing, there is a popular racetrack not far from the Pornichet train station. A current race schedule may be found at **Hippodrome-Pornichet.fr**.
- Water Sports Rentals: Consider renting a jet ski while here for some extra fun. Several firms such as "Aquajet Pornichet" provide boat and jet ski rentals and other services such as parasailing. Check out **www.Aquajet-Pornichet.com**.
- Guérande: This small town is not directly in Pornichet but is reachable by car or bicycle. This is a historic walled town and is enjoyable to explore.

Traveling to Pornichet:
- Train: There are two stations which service Pornichet and this popular beach area. Both are a walk of 8 to 10 minutes to the beaches, but both train stops are serviced by the local bus systems. There are also convenient bicycle rental services near each station.

    Gare de Pornichet services the town of Pornichet.

    Gare de la Baule-les Pins. This station is a short distance northwest of Pornichet and a bit further from the beaches.

    Travel time by train is roughly 50 to 55 minutes in each direction. There are several stops along the way. Check the schedules closely as the number of trains are limited with more trains making this run during peak season.
- Driving: A drive from central Nantes takes about 50 minutes which is the same as taking the train. There are several parking lots, "Parking Avenues," in and near Pornichet, but they can fill up quickly in peak season.

~ ~ ~ ~ ~ ~

Saint-Nazaire:

Saint-Nazaire offers a very different set of opportunities over the previously described Pornic and Pornichet. This is a small city with substantial shipping and industrial activity. When coming here, not only can you visit several attractive beaches, but also consider taking tours of a submarine base, an AirBus factory, prehistoric monuments, and even a shipyard tour.

Beach park at Saint-Nazaire

Located at the mouth of the Loire River, Saint-Nazaire has a long history of fishing, shipping, ship building, and defense. One of the largest ship builders in the world, Chantiers de l'Atlantique, is located here. It has built some of the worlds most noted ships such as the Queen Mary 2 and several modern cruise ships.

It is an easy, small city to visit on a day trip from Nantes by car, bus, or train. The train station is on the northern edge of the

A Starting-Point Guide

town, but local transportation services and bicycle rental are readily available.

Given all that is here, it is advised to check the tourist office's website before coming as you can obtain details on all attractions and even purchase tickets before coming here. The website may be found at **Saint-Nazaire-Tourisme.com**

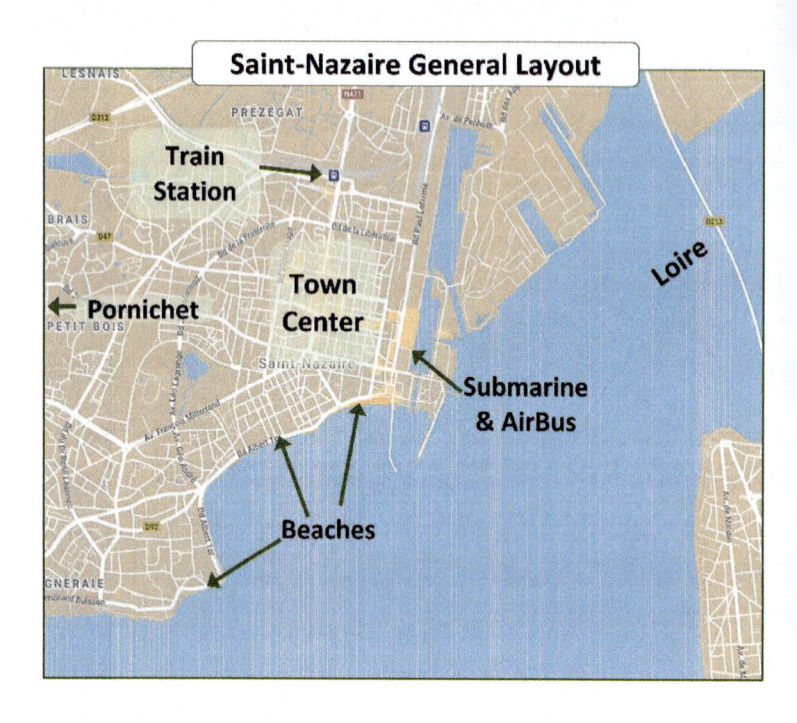

Saint-Nazaire General Layout

Saint-Nazaire Highlights:

- Tourist Office: The Saint-Nazaire tourist office, "Tourist Office of Saint-Nazaire," is located adjacent to the airbus tours along the harbor. Tickets may be purchased here in addition to obtaining a local map of restaurants and attractions.

- Beaches: Saint-Nazaire does have several attractive beaches although these tend to be smaller than those found in

Pornichet, a beach town a short distance west. Of the several beaches nearby, there is also a secluded naturist beach should you forget to bring your bathing suit with you.

The beach closest to town, "La Grande Plage," is right next to the jetty and submarine base. This is an easy and attractive destination to reach on foot or bicycle. Immediately next to this beach is "Plage du Petit Traict." This isanother long stretch which includes rocky areas which can be fun for finding crabs and other small sea life.

- Ecomusée: This combined history and eco museum provides expansive exhibits on the town's industrial past and development. Details may be found at **Saint-Nazaire-Tourisme.com**

- Saint-Nazaire Submarine Base: (Base sous-Marine de Saint-Nazaire). A retired WWII submarine base built by Nazi Germany which is open for tours. When making this tour, you can add on a visit to a French submarine which had played an important role during the cold war of the 1960s.

- AirBus Tours: A large assembly building sits next to the submarine base. Guided tours, 2-hour duration, enable visitors to see how large sections of aircraft are assembled. Tours require advance reservations which may be done via the Saint-Nazaire tourist office.

Traveling to Saint-Nazaire:
- Train: Trains between Nantes and Saint-Nazaire are frequent and travel time is typically only 35 to 45 minutes, depending on the train you take. The station, Gare Saint-Nazaire, is a 10-minute walk into the central shopping district and a 25-minute walk to the area where major attractions such as the popular beach La Grande Plage or the submarine base are.

City buses from the station are frequent and, unless you have rented a bicycle, should be considered. A bicycle rental station is available at the train station.

- Driving: A drive from central Nantes takes about 45 to 50 minutes, slightly longer than taking the train. A great advantage to driving is it provides the ability to easily drive over the impressive bridge, "Pont de Saint-Nazaire," to the south shore where there are numerous attractive beaches and villages to explore.

Vannes:

Vannes is a historical treasure in the Brittany area of France and provides visitors with a wonderful variety of sight-seeing opportunities. It is not directly on the ocean, so beach opportunities are few. Between the city and ocean is the large Gulf of Morbihan which is a popular boating area.

The historic city of Vannes

Vannes General Layout

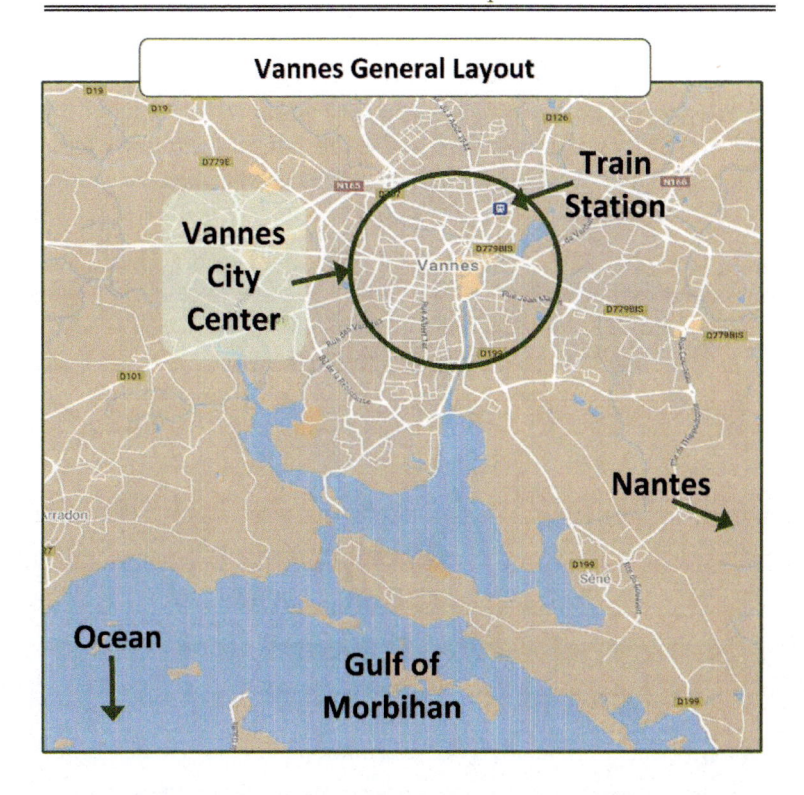

Vannes is known for its medieval town with an impressive city wall. Many of the buildings here are half-timbered and date to the 15th and 16th centuries. The center of town is ideal for strolling.

A good place to start explorations is from the attractive harbor and marina at the southern end of the historic center. From here, you can stroll through ancient city gates and into the maze of streets which define much of the town. Once in the heart of town you have several notable places to visit ranging from the Museum of Archeology to the impressive Château Gaillard.

There is a lot to see here, so obtaining a map from the Tourist Office which sits along the marina is recommended.

A Starting-Point Guide

Vannes Highlights:

- Remparts de Vannes: Ancient city walls which surrounds much of the old town. Just inside the walls are attractive gardens, the "Jarden des Remparts," with the moat running through them.

- Place Henri IV: A historic and very photogenic square located in the heart of town.

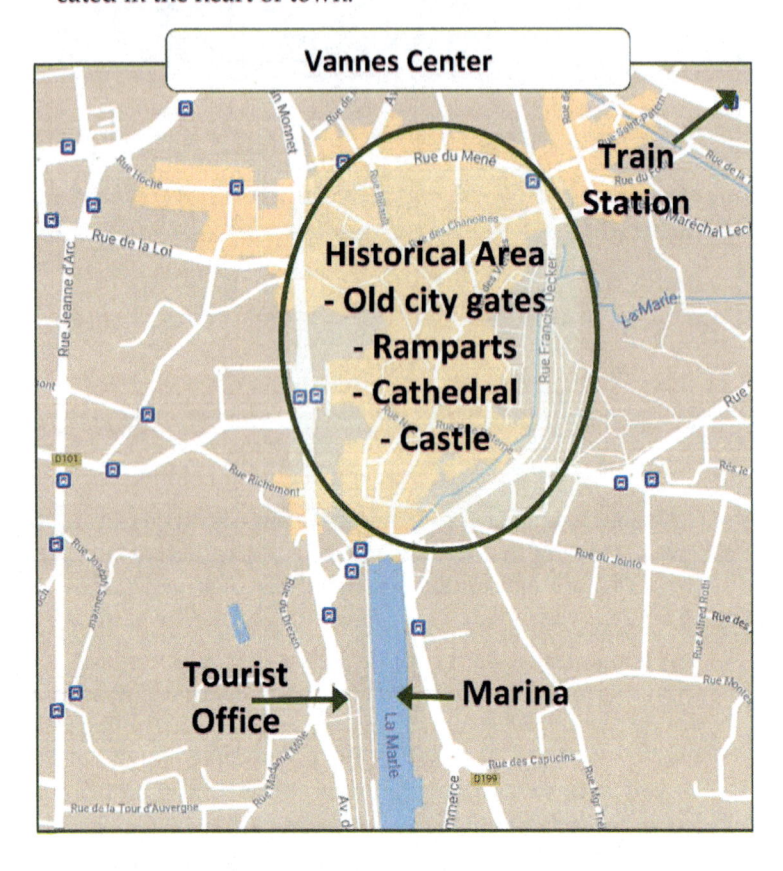

Vannes Center

Train Station

Historical Area
- Old city gates
- Ramparts
- Cathedral
- Castle

Tourist Office

Marina

- Cathedrale Saint-Pierre / Vannes Cathedral: A large Gothic style church which took over 400 years to build and completed in the 19th century. This is a very impressive cathedral to explore and is located in the heart of town.

- Le Port de Plaisance: An attractive marina and harbor which is at the southern end of the heart of town. There are numerous cafes here and it is a popular area for open markets.

Traveling to Vannes:

- Train: Travel time from Nantes is greater than the other towns listed in this chapter. A train trip will take between 75 to 90 minutes each way, depending on the train you select. There are several trains each day which makes travel planning easier, but this is a popular destination so advance booking in the summer months is advised.

  The train station, "Gare de Vannes," is at least a 10-minute walk to the edge of the historic center and roughly 20-minutes to the popular marina area. Buses run frequently from the train station. The town has several bus lines and not all go to the historical center. There is a detailed bus route map at the main bus station which sits across from the train station.

  A bicycle rental station is across from the station and can offer some added fun while visiting this popular town.

- Driving: A drive from central Nantes is 70 kilometers and will take roughly 90 minutes each way. Several parking lots are available in Vannes, but most are a slight distance outside of the historical center.

~ ~ ~ ~ ~ ~

10: Nearby Towns for Great Daytrips

In addition to heading west to the coast, there are several towns of historical significance inland and within easy reach of Nantes. Three of these destinations are outlined in this chapter and they range from a town to the small city of Angers.

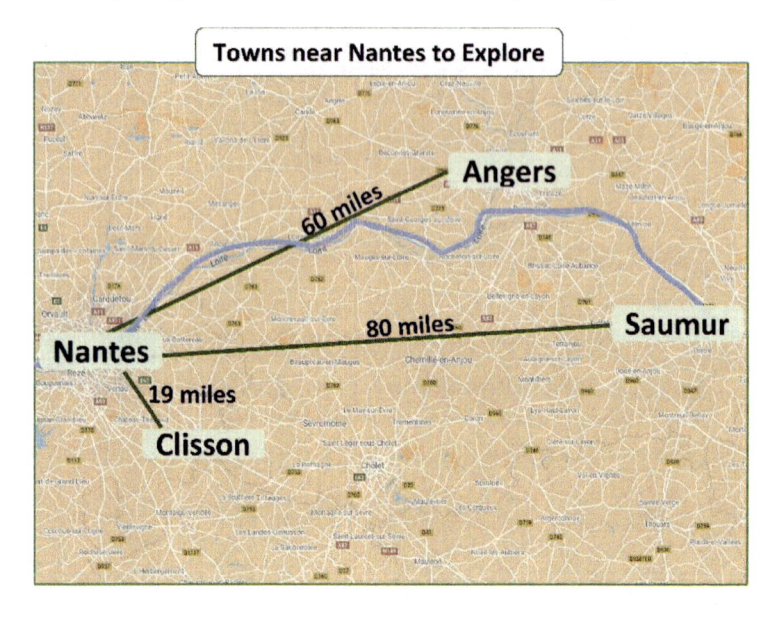

Towns near Nantes to Explore

This guide does not list every place you could visit near Nantes. The focus here is on locations which can be easily reached and explored in one day. They are far from the only enjoyable destinations in the area, but each provides a different atmosphere and set of experiences.

Each of the towns listed here can easily be traveled to by train or car and meet the criteria of:

- Less than 90-minute each way from Nantes.
- The town offers interesting sights and provides pleasant strolling.
- The town has a train station which is convenient to the heart of town and its leading attractions.

Suggested Day Trip from Nantes [9]

Recommended coastal visits are listed in the previous chapter.

Town	Population	Driving Time from central Nantes	Travel Time by Train
Angers	155,000	1hr+	35min+
Clisson	7,000	30min	20min+
Saumur	27,000	1hr & 30min	1hr

---

[9] **Nearby Major Cities**: Cities such as Rennes, Le Mans, and Tours are not included here as they require much more than a simple day trip even though they can be traveled to/from Nantes within a day.

Angers:

A visit to Angers, a city 90km (60 miles) northeast from Nantes, gives the sense of a smaller Nantes. It is an easy city to explore on foot. It sits along the Maine River and near the confluence with the Loire River. The focal point of this town is an impressive chateau, not unlike the one found in Nantes.

Château d'Angers / Angers Castle
Photo Source: Marc Ryckaert - Wikimedia Commons

Similarities to Nantes aside, coming here gives the visitor a good mix of experiences ranging from exploring the numerous plazas, the 9th century Château d'Angers, and the maze of streets lined with shops and restaurants. Much of the center of the city was established and developed in the Middle Ages and this character is readily apparent as you explore the town.

This is an active college town with over 30,000 full-time students enrolled in four colleges including the University of Angers. The large student population gives the area a youthful and vibrant feel.

Daytrips to Nearby Towns

A great place to start explorations is the "Place du Ralliement" in the center of town. Lining the "Place" is the Grand Theater and it has been a major meeting place for centuries. From here, it is a short stroll to the top sights such as the Chateau, the cathedral, and the Beaux Arts Museum. The local tram service stops here making it an easy destination to reach.

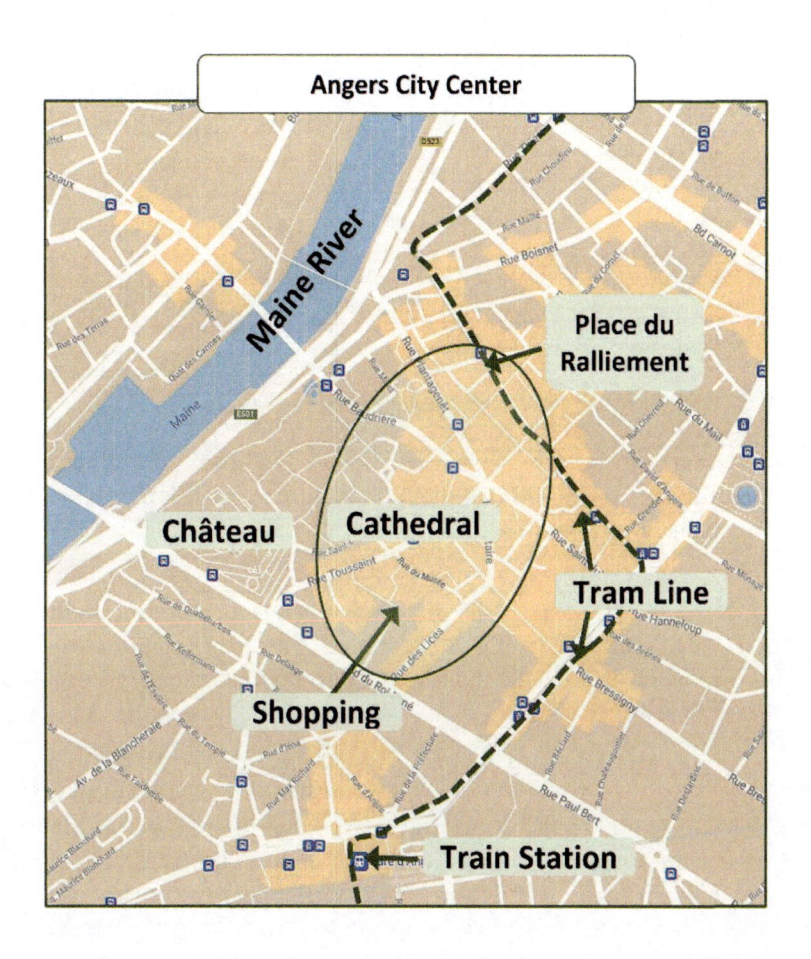

Angers City Center

- Place du Ralliement
- Château
- Cathedral
- Tram Line
- Shopping
- Train Station

Angers Highlights:

- Angers Castle and Apocalypse Tapestry: The large Chateau d'Angers was founded in the 9th century and finished in the 13th century. Overlooking the River Maine, it is easy to see how this location was an excellent location for a fortress.

  This castle and fortress was occupied by the Nazis in WWII. One unfortunate occurrence from this was an ammunition cache in the fortress that exploded and destroyed a large section.

  Today, this is an active museum and holds an amazing set of tapestries known as the Apocalypse Tapestry. Crafted in the 14th century, this large wool tapestry is over 330 feet long and almost 15 feet high.

> **Angers Visitor Website**
>
> The tourist office's website provides an excellent level of information on attractions in and near the city. You may also purchase a local city pass from this site.
>
> **Tourisme.Destination-Angers.com**

- Angers Cathedral / Cathédrale Saint-Maurice: A short walk from the chateau is the impressive Angers Cathedral. Built between the 11th and 16th centuries, this 253ft tall structure reflects different elements of the Baroque, Romanesque, and Renaissance styles.

- Fine Arts Museum / Musée des Beaux-Arts: With the long history of Angers, it is only natural that the art museum would have a rich collection of art and artifacts. The history of the town and area is fully on display with hundreds of items from the 14th century to current times. The museum is in in the heart of town and easy to locate. For full details, check **Musees.Angers.fr**.

Traveling to Angers:

- Train: A train trip from Nantes takes between 35 to 45 minutes each way and there are numerous daily departures. Once you arrive in Angers, consider taking the tram into the center of town. There is a tram station at the Angers train station and there is only 1 line, so it is an easy system to learn. The tram station at Place du Ralliement is in the heart of town and is an easy walk to most attractions and shopping. If you prefer to walk into town, it is a 10- to 15-minute walk, depending on your destination.

- Driving: A drive from Nantes takes slightly over one hour. The trip is mostly along a major highway, and the distance is approximately 98km (61 miles). Once you arrive in Angers, consider going to the parking lot adjacent to the Château d'Angers. This parking lot is also a short walking distance into the heart of the city.

Clisson:

Escape the city and head south to the town of Clisson, a quiet locale sitting along the La Sèvre Nantaise River, a tributary of the Loire. This is not a town with numerous historic buildings or museums. There is one large chateau which makes this jaunt down from Nantes worth doing.

An interesting curiosity about Clisson is that it was purposefully built in an Italian style. Much of the town was crafted in the 19th century to give it an Italian feel by a noted sculptor for Napoleon.

In addition to exploring the chateau and surrounding grounds, a walk over the river on the Pont de la Vallée provides excellent photo opportunities (see above picture). Once across the river, there are restaurants with outdoor seating and views of the chateau.

A Starting-Point Guide

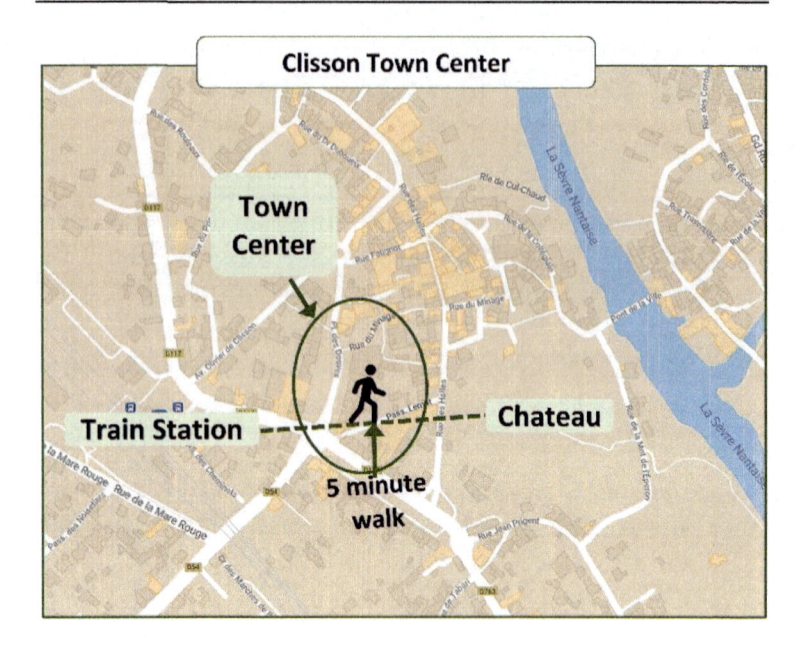

Clisson Town Center

[Map showing Town Center, Train Station, and Chateau with a 5 minute walk indicated]

For some added fun and adventure, consider renting a canoe or kayak while here. A rental firm is an easy 10-minute walk south from the chateau. Areas of the river which different abilities are available.

Clisson Highlights:

- Clisson Castle / Château de Clisson: This imposing fortress was built in the 11th through 17th centuries making it a thousand years old. It is on a high point overlooking the river below and dominates the surrounding area. The castle is open every day except Tuesday and it is an easy walk from town and the train station.

- La Pont de la Vallée: A unique bridge spanning the La Sèvre Nantaise River. Consider crossing the bridge to have lunch at the outdoor restaurant in the Best Western Hotel which faces the river.

- Medieval Market Place / Les Halles de Clisson: A large 15th century timbered marketplace which is still active. Fridays are the best time to visit.

Château de Clisson
Overlooking La Sèvre Nantaise River

Traveling to Clisson:

- Train: This is an easy train trip from Nantes with travel time between 20 to 30 minutes each way. There are numerous daily departures. Once you arrive in Clisson, there is no need for additional transportation unless you are mobility impaired. It is a short 5-minute walk over to the chateau, the main sight in town. Signs clearly mark the way to the chateau.

- Driving: A drive from Nantes takes about 30 minutes and there are several routes to select from. Once in town, there is a large parking lot at the base of the chateau. This parking area is also convenient to both the town and the river front.

~ ~ ~ ~ ~ ~

Saumur:

Château de Saumur
Overlooking the Loire River

Saumur is a scenic medieval town which carries the nickname "The Pearl of Anjou." The large town of 27,000 sits on the Loire River and is a great jumping off location for exploring the famous Loire Valley chateaux and vineyards.

There are many notable historic buildings to explore here, with the most prominent being the castle "Château de Saumur." This impressive structure sits on a bluff overlooking the town. In addition to the chateau, there is a large cathedral and several museums to explore.

Saumur Visitor Website

The tourist office's website provides information on attractions in and near the city including wine and chateau tours.

OT-Saumur.fr

Daytrips to Nearby Towns

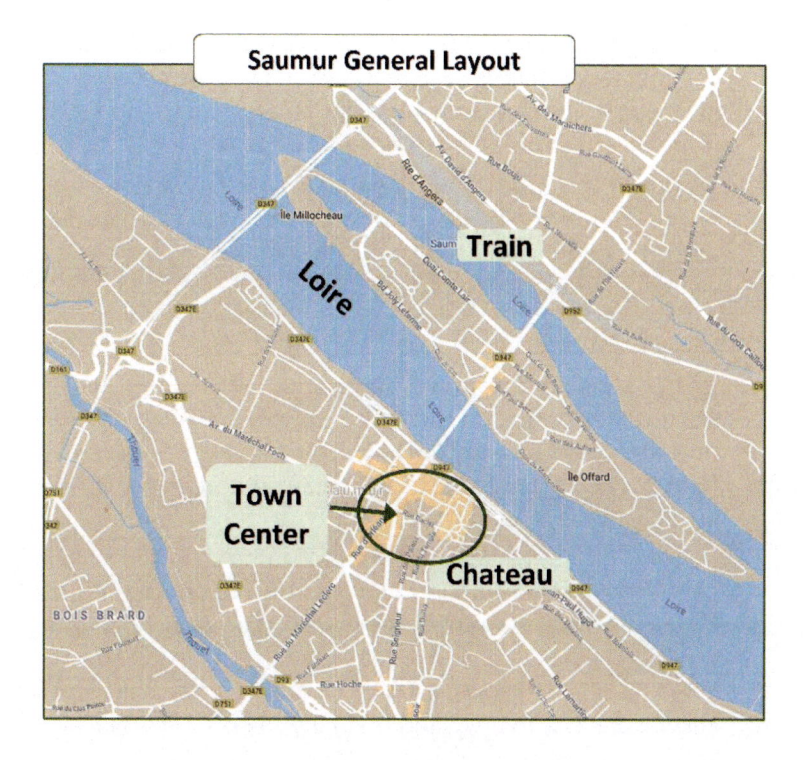

Saumur General Layout

There are many streets to explore in the center of town and along the river front. Allow for a full day when coming here from Nantes or consider spending a couple nights here and taking some of the available tours to the Loire Valley.

Saumur Highlights:

- Château de Saumur: Built in the 10th century as a castle and fortress against Norman attacks. This imposing complex has a long history including being a prison under Napoleon. Today visitors may tour much of the building including the dungeons and towers. Details may be found at **Chateau-Saumur.fr.**

- Cavalry Museum / Musée de la Cavalerie: Saumur has several unique museums. One of these is a museum devoted to the history of France's cavalry. This museum is a short walk from the center of town. **Musee-Cavalerie.fr**.
- The Little Train: During prime months, the city offers a fun open-air train "Le Petite Train." Departing near the tourist office, this ride takes you through the highlights of the town and neighboring vineyards.

Traveling to Saumur:
- Train: A train trip from Nantes takes between 60 to 90 minutes depending on the train selected. Websites such as **Rome2rio.com** are excellent resources to guide you in which train to select. There are several departures each day, making this an easy round trip.

    Saumur's train station, "Gare de Saumur," is across the Loire River from central Saumur and is not an easy walk. The best ways to travel into town are by taxi or the local bus service. The bus stop next to the station has a posted map to help you select the proper bus. This transportation is available for travel into town and up to the chateau. The Saumur bus system website is **Agglobus.fr**.

    If you choose to walk, it is a 20+-minute trek each way. This walk, while it is along busy streets, does offer the benefit of taking you over the Loire River. Great views of the town and chateau are available from this bridge.
- Driving: A drive from Nantes takes around 90 minutes along major highways. Once in Saumur, there is a large parking lot near the entry to the chateau. If you choose to park in town, there are several parking buildings in the center of town.

~ ~ ~ ~ ~ ~

Index

Amusement Park............ 89
Angers, France............... 108
Apps to Download............ 4
Bicycle Rentals................. 53
Bon Voyage Pass 36
Botanical Garden............. 60
Chateau du Coing 84
Christmas Market............ 23
City Pass 36
City Tour Bus................... 51
Climate by Month 20
Clisson, France............... 111
Coastal Towns 91
Events in Nantes 22
Fine Arts Museum 58
Gare de Nantes 17
History of Nantes............ 13
Hotel Guide...................... 24
Jules Verne Museum....... 69
La Maison du Lac........... 86
Le Grand Elephant.......... 71
Les Machines 71
Nantes Airport................. 17
Nantes Castle 62
Nantes Cathedral 65
Nantes Introduction.......... 6
Natural History Museum
.... 75
Naval Museum 77
Passage Pommeraye 79
Pornic, France 93
Pornichet, France............. 96
River Shuttle 49
Saint-Nazaire, France...... 99
Saumur, France.............. 114
Slavery Museum.............. 73
Talensac Market 81
Tourist Office 2
Train Station..................... 17
Tram System 47
Transportation System ... 45
Traveling to Nantes......... 16
Vannes, France............... 102
Zen Garden 67

Starting-Point Guides

www.StartingPointGuides.com

This guidebook on Nantes is one of several current and planned **Starting-Point Guides**. Each book in the series is developed with the concept of using one enjoyable city as your basecamp and then exploring from there.

Current guidebooks are for:

- **Bordeaux, France** and the surrounding Gironde River region.
- **Dijon, France** and the Burgundy Region.
- **Geneva, Switzerland** and the Lake Geneva Area.
- **Gothenburg, Sweden** and the Västra Götaland region.
- **Lille, France** and the Nord-Pas-de-Calais Area.
- **Lucerne, Switzerland** and the Lake Lucerne area.
- **Lyon, France** and the Saône and Rhône confluence area.
- **Strasbourg, France** and the central Alsace region.
- **Stuttgart, Germany** and the Baden-Württemberg area.
- **Toulouse, France** and the Haute-Garonne district.

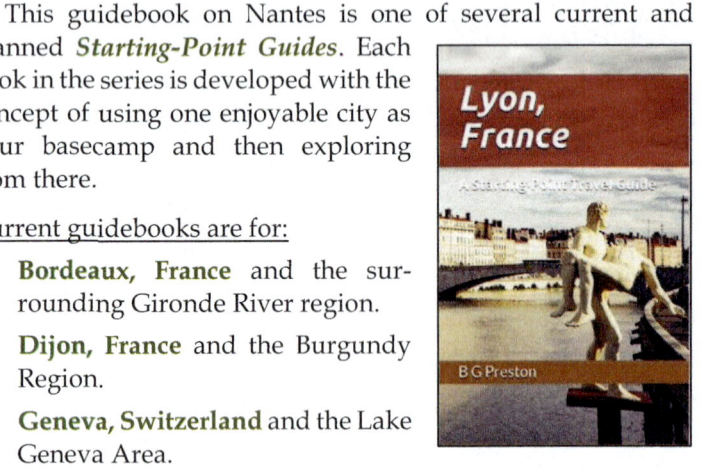

~ ~ ~ ~ ~

Updates on these and other titles may be found on the author's Facebook page at:

www.Facebook.com/BGPreston.author

Feel free to use this Facebook page to provide feedback and suggestions to the author or email to: cincy3@gmail.com

Printed in Great Britain
by Amazon